"Megan Smolenyak is a blessing to cold case detectives and a master genealogist."

—Julie M. Haney, special agent,
NCIS Cold Case Homicide Unit

"Megan Smolenyak manages to make this book a fun, informative read while still filling it with information. The tales are illuminating, fascinating, and in some cases, heartbreaking. Megan solves genealogical mysteries with a combination of humanity, empathy, and skill that makes for a great read."

—Tara Calishain, co-author of *Googles Hacks* and
editor/writer of the ResearchBuzz blog

"The authors are smart . . . Their book offers a comprehensive overview of a frontier that no website currently offers. It is a wonderful portal to this coming century."

—Kevin Kelly, co-founder of *Wired*, on *Trace Your
Roots with DNA*, co-authored with Ann Turner

"I loved it! Thanks so much."

—Malcolm Gladwell, on an article Megan
Smolenyak wrote about the genealogical
aspects of his bestselling book *Outliers*

"Megan Smolenyak's unusual ability to find living relatives of deceased individuals assists coroners and medical examiners with the critical task of next-of-kin notification. Her skills in tracking down families, however remote and distant, are amazing."

—Gretchen Geary, Medical Examiner
Investigator, San Diego

"Megan Smolenyak is the genealogist's genealogist: the go-to person for building your family tree and solving stubborn historical mysteries."

—Dr. Spencer Wells, director of the Genographic Project, National Geographic Explorer-in-Residence, and author of *Journey of Man: A Genetic Odyssey*

"No one but Megan Smolenyak could have written this book. The Indiana Jones of genealogy, Smolenyak's passion for cracking historical mysteries is on full display here. Many people daydream about tracking down their ancestors; a small subset of those actually make a few stabs at research; but Megan Smolenyak takes it to the nth degree, using paper trails, oral histories, and DNA to unlock the door of the past. Whether it's reconstructing the lives of long-forgotten tenant farmers or re-contextualizing the family history of world leaders, Smolenyak's sleuthing reveals that, in fact, all these lives are connected. Anyone interested in genealogy or in the history of this country will love this book. Smolenyak teaches Americans something important: it's good to let your roots show! Megan Smolenyak is a national treasure."

—Buzzy Jackson, author of *Shaking the Family Tree*

"No one is better than Megan Smolenyak at finding—and getting to the bottom of—history's mysteries. Once she latches on to a subject, she doesn't let go until she's turned up every shred of hard evidence. And she makes the search itself more compelling than any detective thriller. In this sensational book, Megan invites us along as she excavates the past for incredible stories and champions those who've been overlooked by history. She is, hands down, America's greatest genealogist, and this book is proof of it."

—Andrew Carroll, editor of the *New York Times* bestsellers *War Letters* and *Behind the Lines*

Hey, America, Your Roots Are Showing

*Adventures in Discovering
News-Making Connections,
Unexpected Ancestors,
Long-Hidden Secrets, and
Solving Historical Puzzles*

MEGAN SMOLENYAK²

FOREWORD BY HENRY LOUIS GATES, JR.

CITADEL PRESS
Kensington Publishing Corp.
www.kensingtonbooks.com

CITADEL PRESS BOOKS are published by

Kensington Publishing Corp.
119 West 40th Street
New York, NY 10018

All Kensington titles, imprints, and distributed lines are available at special quantity discounts for bulk purchases for sales promotions, premiums, fundraising, educational, or institutional use. Special book excerpts or customized printings can also be created to fit specific needs. For details, write or phone the office of the Kensington special sales manager: Kensington Publishing Corp., 119 West 40th Street, New York, NY 10018, attn: Special Sales Department; phone 1-800-221-2647.

CITADEL PRESS and the Citadel logo are Reg. U. S. Pat. & TM Off.

First printing: February 2012

10 9 8 7 6 5 4 3 2

Printed in the United States of America

CIP data is available.

ISBN-13: 978-0-8065-3446-6
ISBN-10: 0-8065-3446-X

For Brian—I'd wait another 40 years for you!
For Stacy—simply the best sister in the world ever.
And for Annie, Melvina, Fulmoth, Coleman, Hinda,
Philip, and Mabel—welcome back.

Contents

Foreword

HENRY LOUIS GATES, JR.
The Alphonse Fletcher University Professor

The great philosopher Isaiah Berlin, drawing upo
Greek poet Archilochus's witty observation that "the fox knows
many little things, but the hedgehog knows one big thing," fa-
mousl   orld's great thinkers into those two cate-
gories: hedgehogs (including Plato, Dante, Hegel, Dostoevsky,
Nietzsche, Ibsen, Proust), interpret things through one overarch-
ing idea while foxes (Aristotle, Shakespeare, Goethe, Pushkin,
Joy   subjects from a variety of perspectives, es-
chew a single interpretive framework as they write about ideas.

We can, perhaps, draw upon Berlin's distinction when we
think about the talents of genealogists. Since producing and
hosting the popular PBS series *African American Lives* and *Faces of
America*, it has been my pleasure to work with a few truly great
genealogists. And one of these is Megan Smolenyak. Megan is,
without question, a fox, if we modify Berlin's classification a bit
for the kinds of genealogists at work today in this ever-expanding
field. Consider the following sentence, taken from one of the
chapters in this book and you will see what I mean:

> As it was, I e-mailed a friend in Jerusalem, who called a
> cousin in Cairo, who forwarded some googled links to me
> in New Jersey, which I then shared with an American
> cousin in Poland, who passed them on to a professor in

> Cairo, who shot the translations to me back in New Jersey, where I facebooked my way to Hoda's cousin, who digitized some wonderful family photos—all in the space of one week so that I could have something semi-intelligent to say about Hoda's remarkable heritage on the *Today* show. Phew!

And "Phew!" is right! I know of *very* few, if any, genealogists who are as adept at the traditional painstaking sort of genealogical research in dusty archives and this sort of speed-of-light research enabled by the Internet. As Megan also says, "Admittedly, this isn't conventional genealogy, but family history is constantly evolving, and social networking is one of the newer tools we now have at our disposal. Had all this happened a decade ago, I probably would have been out of luck.—" She is being characteristically modest: few genealogists have mastered these new tools of social networking as thoroughly as Megan has. When I need a quick answer to a perplexing problem about someone's family tree, Megan's is the e-mail address that I summon first.

I can give you an example. A few months ago, I was correcting the galleys of a new edition of Jean Toomer's classic black novel of the Harlem Renaissance, entitled *Cane*, which I edited with my friend and colleague Rudolph Byrd, a dis███████████lar at Emory University. The novel was initially published in 1922, and Professor Byrd and I were publishing a new edition in the Norton Critical Edition series. Toomer wrote this brilliant book identifying himself as a black man, then he decided to pass for white. But when he decided to pass for white, he also concocted an outrageous and highly suspicious story that his black grandfather, P.B.S. Pinchback, the first black lieutenant governor of Louisiana (and of any state), was actually a white man who, for opportunistic reasons, passed for black! It occurred to me, in the middle of the night, that we could check how Pinchback was

identified on any public record listing race during his lifetime, between his birth in 1837 and his death in 1921, including census
records and his death certificate. I e-mailed Megan first thing the
next morning. Within minutes, literally, she had confirmed my
theory that Pinchback—and every other member of Toomer's
family tree on this line—were also identified as black or mulatto
in all extant public records. Only Toomer and an aunt decided to
pass. Armed with this new information, which had just been sitting in the archives, waiting for a scholar to discover it, we could
establish beyond the shadow of a doubt that Jean Toomer was a
black man who passed for white.

This is only one example of many. The strength of genealogy
is also its weakness, as I have discovered over the past decade,
preparing the family trees of the guests in my various PBS series:
anyone can do it, which means that unlike the academy, it is not
adequately supervised. Results can be highly dubious, especially
results deduced from false cognates, as it were—that is, to assume someone is an ancestral relation because of a similar
name. Or to leap to a conclusion based on a concrete detail about
an ancestor, such as assuming Native American genetic admixture for the descendant of black slaves owned by the Chickasaw,
as in the case of my guest Don Cheadle. That would seem to be a
reasonable conclusion, or "common sense"—don't you think?—
given the fact that Cheadle's family was owned by various Chickasaw masters between the Trail of Tears in the 1830s and the
statehood of Oklahoma in 1907. Turns out, though, that Cheadle has o percent Native American genetic admixture! One
learns, painfully, that there are genealogists too eager to uncover
roots that have no branches, to paraphrase the great black femi-
nist novelist Zora Neale Hurston. Would that all genealogists had
that rarest of attributes, the combined skills of the hedgehog and
the fox, skills that characterize the work of Megan Smolenyak,
and which she draws upon to make genealogy come alive in the
most vivid and compelling manner in this splendid book. It is

essential reading for all of us who love family history and who understand the deep and abiding pleasures of introducing our friends and clients to their virtual ancestors.

Harvard University
February 20, 2011

Hey, America, Your Roots Are Showing

Rewriting History

Have you noticed that history is being rewritten? Oh, it's early days yet, but our current, somewhat patchy perspective is gradually giving way to a more nuanced and refined understanding of our collective past. We've all heard that history is written by the victors, which is certainly true, but it's also written by the wealthy and the literate. A high profile position has always worked in your favor if you hoped to leave a legacy, but having money and the means to record your own thoughts undoubtedly enhanced your odds. That's why we all grow up learning about generals and presidents in school, and why so much of what we "know" is the story of gentlemen of leisure, even if their lives were less than leisurely.

When I say this, I don't mean to belittle the accomplishments of those whose names we memorize for tests and whose statues we admire. I just think it's time to make a little room for the rest of our ancestors—and I'm happy to report that this is already happening. You never had to be famous, rich, or educated to leave a trace, but unless you were, you tended to be over-looked. But now, that's all beginning to change, and at the vanguard of this democratization of history is the humble genealogist.

Every genealogist is fascinated by those who came before, and to us, the ancestral peasant is as intriguing as the colonial governor who adorns the family tree (and frankly, the so-called black sheep can often be even more interesting). And though that peasant may have been unable to read or write, he probably left a trail of historical bread crumbs in church, census, military, labor, and other records. Genealogists follow those trails, each one of us pursuing dozens or even hundreds of ancestors, and there are millions of us with our numbers growing by the day. So do the math. The lives of countless everyman types are finally being recovered and shared, and with each one, our grasp of our past is coming more sharply into focus. I think of each story as adding another pixel to the overall picture of our past and bringing greater clarity. If knowing the tales of generals and presidents provides a 72 dpi impression, injecting the rest of our forebears into the mix will slowly but steadily take us into the realm of high definition.

I'm a sucker for the historical underdog, so this delights me to no end. I've always found myself drawn to the neglected—those whose lives and contributions have been ignored, undervalued or dismissed—so it's become something of a mission of mine to shine a light on at least a few of these forgotten souls. I've been very fortunate in this mission with some of my discoveries making front-page news, while other beneath-the-radar findings have had a profound effect on a select few.

I also like to push the boundaries of conventional genealogy, seeking unexpected applications that can be surprisingly relevant in today's world. That explains why I was one of the first to play with DNA—and when I say "play," I mean just that. I'm one of those obnoxious people you hear about from time to time who has the privilege of making a living doing what she loves. As a real-life history detective, I wake up excited every day about what I'm going to tackle and what I might uncover.

In this book, I'd like to take you into my world and essentially perch you on my shoulder to see how it's done. How did I figure out who would be king of America today if George Washington had been king instead of president? How did I come to work with the FBI and NCIS on cold cases and with coroners' offices to find relatives of unclaimed people? How did I unravel the mystery of a Hebrew-inscribed tombstone found on the streets of Manhattan? How did I successfully trace Michelle Obama's roots when others had tried but gotten roadblocked early on? How did I research Hoda Kotb's Egyptian heritage in no time flat for a *Today* show appearance? How did I use DNA to learn that the Haley family of *Roots* fame is Scottish?

This book includes more than twenty of my favorite investigatory romps, all of which extended my understanding of our history in some way. Following the path of a Bible that traded hands during the Civil War gave me a fresh perspective from both the Confederate and Union viewpoints. My first case with the FBI was an in-your-face education about the civil rights movement. And pursuing the real Annie Moore, first to arrive at Ellis Island (whose place had been usurped by an impostor), informed my understanding of the tenement life so many of our immigrant ancestors endured.

Given my proclivity for resurrecting the historically neglected, it's no accident that many of the chapters in this book feature women and African Americans—both harder to research, but all the more rewarding because of it. So I'll introduce you to everyone from Mabel Cavin Sills Leish Whitworth Davis, a partially paralyzed prostitute (yes, you read that right) who taught me about the realities of life in a Western mining community, to Philip Reed, the slave behind the installment of the Freedom statue on top of the Capitol dome.

Along the way, you'll also find a healthy dose of my opinions, so consider yourself forewarned if you still believe your name was changed at Ellis Island!

It is my hope that by the end of this book, you will find yourself looking at some aspect of our history a little differently than you did at the outset—and better yet, feel compelled to reach into the past and contribute a few pixels yourself. It's high time for all of us to let our roots show!

CHAPTER ONE

No Man Left Behind (for Real)

A decade of forensic consulting for the Army

OF ALL THE RESEARCH I've done to date, perhaps the most important is the forensic genealogy I do in conjunction with the repatriation efforts of the Joint POW/MIA Accounting Command (JPAC). Though many don't realize it, "no man left behind" is much more than an expression. The U.S. military genuinely does all it can to recover soldiers from all conflicts, and over the past decade, I've had the privilege of helping solve cases pertaining to WWI, WWII, Korea, and Southeast Asia.

As an army brat whose father served in Vietnam, I can't think of any more meaningful work. It gives me a deep sense of satisfaction each time one of "my boys" is identified and buried. (I tend to get a little possessive, and even though it's tempting to think of the soldiers as old men since they mostly lived and died before I was born, I remind myself that the majority barely made it past their teens.) I've had the opportunity to visit JPAC's facility in Hawaii, and on the walls, there are large plaques with rows of gold faceplates engraved with the names of those who have been identified. Gazing at them and recognizing so many names is one of my best memories.

The perennial research boot camp this initiative provides is largely responsible for sharpening my skills and making me the sleuth I am today. In Malcolm Gladwell's *Outliers*, he cites the ten-thousand-hour rule—the notion that once you've done something for that many hours, you tend to get pretty darn good at it. I'm blessed to have started genealogy in the sixth grade, but thanks to the effort I've put into locating thousands of family members for the army, I've gotten even better. The repatriation project gives me the chance to flex my search muscles every day with cases that take me to every corner of America (not to mention a number of other countries) and expose me to family dynamics I never could have imagined. When you research thousands of people, you're bound to confront a stunning array of human drama, and because of that, these cases keep me humble as a genealogist. Just when I think I've seen it all, they throw me curves I never could have dreamed of. And because I'm the one who locates and cold-calls my way into the lives of soldiers' families, I've evolved into a hybrid genealogist/detective, as good at finding the living as the dearly departed.

This work has also served as the springboard for so much more I've gone on to do, such as establishing Unclaimed Persons, a volunteer organization that assists coroners, and helping the FBI and NCIS with cold cases (more on both of these in upcoming chapters)—but I'm getting a bit ahead of myself.

What's JPAC?

Did you know that roughly 75,000 Americans are unaccounted for from WWII, and another 8,000 from Korea and 1,700 from Vietnam? You can add still others from WWI and Cold War days, but unless these figures include someone from your family, there's a good chance you haven't heard of JPAC.

Headquartered in Hawaii, its mission is to "achieve the fullest possible accounting of all Americans missing as a result of the nation's past conflicts."

Some four hundred–people strong, it consists of personnel from all American armed forces and some of the most highly respected forensic anthropologists in the world. Every year, JPAC teams scour the globe for remains and effects of soldiers from past conflicts in conditions that resemble episodes of *Man vs. Wild*. Any given expedition might center on a mountaintop in India, a swampy region in Vietnam, or the jungles of Papua New Guinea, and whatever is found is brought to the Central Identification Laboratory on the island of Oahu for processing and analysis.

Many factors go into identification. Location is key. For instance, if an excavation takes place at the site of a former POW camp or plane crash, historical documents can furnish a short list of candidates. Buttons, heels of boots, or countless other items that might be recovered are examined. Skeletal remains are carefully scrutinized for clues about size, age, ethnicity, previous injuries, and so forth. Teeth, if found, are compared against soldiers' dental records. And as you might suspect, DNA—using reference samples supplied by soldiers' relatives—is also used. That's where I come in.

PNOK and mtDNA

I'm afraid JPAC was just a warm-up when it comes to the alphabet soup aspect of this work, so please bear with me as I introduce the concept of PNOK. When I handle a case, it's my responsibility to find the PNOK, or "primary next of kin," the individual officially considered to be the soldier's closest living relative. To this end, there's a strict hierarchy involving spouses, children, parents (in the early days, I would still find the occasional 100-year-old mother of a Korean War soldier alive), siblings, cousins, and beyond. Should any effects be found, this is the person who will receive them, and should any remains be identified, this is the person who will make the burial decisions.

In addition to locating the PNOK, I'm responsible for locating at least three living relatives with the same mitochondrial DNA (mtDNA) as the soldier. Mitochondrial DNA is passed maternally. In a nutshell, mothers transmit it to both their sons and daughters, but their sons don't pass it on. So if, for instance, a soldier from the Korean War had a brother and sister who are both alive, either could provide a reference sample to help identify him. But if both siblings have passed on, the sister's children can give mtDNA samples, but the brother's cannot.

Though Y-DNA (passed paternally from father to son down through the generations) can be used in exceptional cases, this is a recent development and one that still offers somewhat iffy prospects at this time. Mitochondrial DNA is plentiful, and therefore quite resilient. Even in degraded remains, it tends to survive in sufficient quantities to test, so it is the preferred type of DNA for most cases. This results in research that disproportionately emphasizes the maternal half of a soldier's family, and that can be rather challenging since most women's surnames change upon marriage. But with a solution rate that hovers around 95 percent, I can confidently say that there's almost always someone alive with the right DNA to help identify any given soldier.

Why Genealogy?

With all the anthropological, archaeological, dental, linguistic, forensic, and other experts working for JPAC, why is there a need for genealogists as well? Well, to begin with, the paper trail isn't what you might expect. Back in 1973, a fire (along with the water used to extinguish it) destroyed a significant portion of American military personnel records from the twentieth century up to that point. The army was hardest hit with roughly 85 percent of its records damaged or consumed. That's especially regrettable since the majority of those who remain unaccounted for—particularly from the Korean War—served in the army.

For that reason, most of my cases start with skimpy information—the name and birth date of the soldier, the county he enlisted from, and the name and address of someone associated with him (maybe parents, wife, siblings, or friends) at the time he joined. That's about it. Even with the simplest of cases, decades have passed and relatives have died. It's a given that I will encounter at least these factors, but most cases entail a variety of other roadblocks and detours.

One of these is the fact that Americans have been on the move for centuries. With Vietnam cases, I'm dealing with a forty plus year gap, and with most of my Korean War cases (the largest share of my work), I'm researching soldiers born around the late 1920s based on a few tidbits from the late 1940s. Now ponder our recent history for a bit. Dust bowl migration. The Great Migration. Katrina. Each one of these scrambled people around the country, and that's before we consider the coal miners who left Pennsylvania for auto jobs in Michigan or their children who left Michigan the following generation for jobs in the oil industry in Texas. Then there are the New Yorkers who retire to Florida for a warmer climate or the Californians who retire to Oregon for a lower cost of living. Of course, I can't forget the career military families (like the one I grew up in) that bounce from place to place every few years. Every once in a great while, I find someone in a soldier's family still living at the same address that they (or more likely, their parents) did in 1948, but that's a much-celebrated exception. However you look at it, we are a remarkably mobile society.

Having conducted or orchestrated research in many countries, I can also say that the United States is quite complicated compared to most. Whereas many countries have centralized vital records, for example, each of our states maintains its own birth, marriage, and death records. We were relative latecomers to the establishment and maintenance of such records, and just for fun, each state has its own set of laws determining who's entitled to copies of those records. Many of these rules have become more restrictive since 9/11 and due to growing concerns about privacy, and I've spent untold hours requesting, pleading, cajoling, and campaigning for copies of documents that might help solve a case. I've found that it can be easier to secure a copy of a particular record from Sweden than from Maryland, and I'm not above faxing a state governor or senator for assistance in gaining access to a birth certificate that might help me find a soldier's family.

While I'm on this topic, I might as well answer the question I get all the time: Yes, Hawaii is exceedingly tight with its records. Barack Obama's birth certificate is not treated any differently from any others. I have never succeeded in getting a copy of the birth certificate of a Hawaiian-born soldier, even though my requests are being made on behalf of the federal government and I can prove that the individual in question is long deceased. Some states have inexplicably restrictive laws and refuse to make exceptions for anyone or any reason. One state's department of health (not Hawaii) made it clear that they were quite proud to have rejected the request made by one of their senators to help solve the case of a soldier from their state. I find that attitude perplexing, but it certainly exists. Having dealt with every state at this point, I know which ones are researcher-friendly and which aren't, and I've developed workarounds for the ones that aren't.

The genealogist is also the one who makes the initial contact with a family. This is necessary to confirm that the family tree I've pieced together through the paper trail is correct, as well as to confirm current contact information for family members. Put yourself in the shoes of those who receive these calls. You have, say, an uncle who was killed in Korea and someone calls out of the blue decades later. How are you going to respond? As you might expect, I get every kind of reaction possible. Many are stunned and grateful, but over the last decade, we've become increasingly wary. When I finally manage to get past the hurdles of multiple addresses and unlisted numbers, I frequently get grilled by those who think I'm a scam artist or a creditor (I always offer an 800 number to call the army to verify that I am who I claim to be, but some prefer to vent instead). From time to time, I get yelled at or hung up on. Some are indifferent and some are still angry. And then there are language issues when a case leads me overseas, where the reason for my call or e-mail sounds stranger still to those I'm contacting. I won't lie; this work requires a thick skin. But for every time I bear the brunt of suspicion or pent-up frustration, there's another when I'm showered with gratitude I don't deserve. And I'm the one who has the pleasure of finding the soldier's twin, ninety-year-old siblings hale and hearty, listening to the fond reminiscences of an elderly person happy to have an audience for their memories of the soldier, occasionally reuniting branches of the family who have lost track of each other, or otherwise receiving or delivering good news.

But perhaps the most important reason to use genealogy is this: you have to be right. With JPAC's critical mission, the involvement of soldiers' families, and the use of DNA testing, accuracy matters. I remember watching a documentary about the *H.L. Hunley*, a Confederate submarine that sank in 1864, and much to my horror they mistakenly disinterred a step-relative—in other words, a person with no blood relationship—in an attempt to identify one of the sailors. While I'm not against disinterment with the aim of solving history mysteries, I think every precaution should be taken to dig up the *right* people! I'm not saying that mistakes are entirely avoidable. You might DNA test a soldier's relative only to later learn (even to the relative's surprise) of a hidden adoption in the family. Quirky situations definitely arise. But every effort must be made to find the true next-of-kin and potential DNA donors, and it's remarkably easy to bark up the wrong family tree. In fact, the ever-exploding plethora of family history resources that has become available in recent years makes it easier than ever to take a misstep by accidentally latching on to the wrong Smith or Jones family, one that just happens to share a lot in common with the soldier's family.

The Family Factor

Speaking of the families, the soldiers themselves and their families are obviously the raison d'être for all this. It's long been said that one of the measures of a civilization is its treatment of its dead, and that's just one of the many reasons I'm so grateful for this "no man left behind" commitment. In terms of genealogy, though, the soldiers' families are representative of the rest of us—and that means that they include every possible circumstance you can imagine.

When I'm lucky, the PNOK and mtDNA candidates overlap. For instance, the soldier's oldest brother or sister might happen to be both, so all I have to do is include a few more siblings or perhaps the children of the sister and I'm done. It sounds straightforward, but rarely is. I can't begin to spell out all the complications that can trip you up, but here's a sampling:

- The soldier was an only child or all his siblings and other close relatives have passed away. (That means I'll wind up reaching out to relatives who have probably never heard of him.)
- His next-of-kin is his oldest brother, but no one's seen him in decades. (Guess who gets to find him?)
- The soldier was adopted or raised in foster care, or his parents were (requiring me to deal with sealed records and other obstacles).
- He's from South Carolina, but enlisted while on vacation in Philadelphia (which wouldn't be a problem if anything in his file indicated that he was from South Carolina, something I'll have to figure out on my own).

- The soldier's name was Henry, but everyone knew him only as Buddy, Junior, or some other nickname (leading to strange conversations where it takes relatives a while to register that I'm calling about the cousin they grew up with).

- The only relative listed is his wife, but there's no sign of her since she remarried into another surname and there's no hint of the soldier's birth family (which essentially doubles the workload since I have to trace both his former spouse and the family he was born into).

- The soldier didn't even know his own mother's name (this sad occurrence makes it considerably more difficult to find mtDNA candidates).

- He was an immigrant and the only one in his family ever to come to America (which translates into adventures with foreign languages and records for me).

- The soldier has plenty of close relatives, but none who share his mtDNA (time to steel myself to dig back several centuries).

- The soldier's parents had half a dozen marriages among them and even his siblings aren't clear on who's a full or half sibling. (It's always fun to sort out what the family itself doesn't know!)

- He lied—about his age, his parents, or even his name (more common than you would expect).

These are some of the more common hiccups. For instance, before Social Security registration truly took hold on a nationwide basis, it was very easy to fib about your age. For that matter, many immigrants didn't know their own birthdays, but the challenge I run into over and over is soldiers who were so patriotic that they lied in order to enter the service underage. Luckily, most of us are unsophisticated liars, so all I usually have to do if I can't find a soldier in birth indexes or records is to look for those born on the same day and month, but one to three years later. Using this tactic, I've discovered soldiers to be as young as fifteen at the time of enlistment.

Over the years, I've bumped into these and countless other hurdles in the course of my research. Of course, protecting the families' privacy is paramount, so to give you a better sense, I'll briefly describe some of my more memorable cases and the unexpected scenarios I've dealt with without disclosing specifics that would point to a particular family.

The Name Game

I've already mentioned that it wasn't unusual for soldiers to round their ages up. That generally presents minimal challenge, but when they lie about their names, it gets trickier. I've only had about half a dozen such cases over the years, but there's no way to know up front that you're dealing with a name-changer. Generally, the discovery is made completely by accident or the hard way, upon the realization that nothing is adding up in spite of exhaustive digging.

I recall one instance when I couldn't get traction on a soldier who should have been easy to find. There were several record sets that should have included him, but didn't. Stumped as to what to do next, I decided to look for others who shared his decidedly Irish-sounding name. When I did this, I couldn't help but notice that one of them lived in Chicago, where he was from. Thinking that this fellow might be a cousin, I gave him a call. That's how I learned that he was the soldier's half brother.

This turned out to be another one of those underage situations. The soldier wanted to enlist, but was too young, so he snagged the birth certificate of his older half brother (same mother, different father, so a different surname as well) and used that to sign up. The family only learned when the half brother whose name he had borrowed happened to be the one at home to receive the telegram declaring the soldier's MIA status. Today it would be exceedingly difficult to enlist under another's name, but in the 1940s, this was much easier than you might suppose, so I have to be open to that possibility.

What Brother?

Because of the nature of this research, I often wind up knowing more about the families I contact than they know themselves, but even I didn't expect to find myself in a situation I've now been in twice. On two separate occasions, I've had to call a septuagenarian and convince them that they had a brother they never knew about who was killed in Korea. In both cases, they had spent their entire lives thinking they were only children, and both handled the startling news very well.

One was a woman whose mother had a son quite young. The son was already in his late teens (on the verge of joining the military) by the time the now seventy-something daughter was born. And for whatever reasons, the mother opted not to tell her second child about the first.

The other case was, in some respects, even more curious. The gentleman I called was the half brother of a soldier he had never heard of. In fact, he and the soldier were born only six months apart (their father apparently had an affair) and both served in Korea, though only the one came home. This half brother wasn't eligible to provide a DNA sample since they had different mothers, but I was able to locate a younger, maternal half brother of the soldier—rather miraculously, as he had recently left the Las Vegas trailer park he lived in for the peace and quiet of Montana—and he, sharing the same mother, had the desired DNA. The sample the younger brother gave helped identify the soldier, but since seniority factors in (both relatives were half brothers, but the paternal one was older), the one who had no previous knowledge of the soldier was declared his next-of-kin.

This worked out beautifully as the younger brother preferred not to have the responsibility, and the older, newfound brother—a fellow Korean War veteran—welcomed the right to make burial decisions. He selected Arlington National Cemetery for his brother's final resting place, and his entire family flew from California to attend the funeral of a relative they had never known—simply because they believed it was the right thing to do.

What Child?

Given what I've just covered about unknown siblings, you probably won't be shocked to hear about unexpected offspring of soldiers. Think about it. A young man is about to go off to war. He meets a beautiful, young woman and... well, you can guess the rest. As a result, I occasionally turn up a child the soldier's birth family has no clue about. I've found them everywhere from New Jersey to Hawaii, and even in Japan.

Whether to share this information with the soldier's family is a delicate matter, but sometimes the purported child can technically be the soldier's next-of-kin, so he or she can't be ignored. I make case-by-case decisions depending on the specifics and personalities of those involved. Upon telling one very matter-of-fact woman in Texas about her previously unknown grandchild in New Jersey, for instance, she immediately and calmly accepted the situation, remarking on the number of "outside children" in her family. There are others where I've chosen to keep mum because it was clear that the information and child would be unwelcome.

At present, I'm working on one of my more astonishing cases, one that involves a soldier who lost his life in Vietnam. German-born, he came to America as a youngster with his mother after his parents divorced. She married and moved several times, and he eventually joined the army. Perhaps the loss of her only child was too much for his mother, so she eventually returned to Germany, never troubling to inform the soldier's father of her return.

Fast-forward a few decades. I received his case and began the usual research—more challenging than most since I had to find his father in Germany and follow his mother on her circuitous journey through multiple states and marriages back to her motherland. Now eighty-eight and ninety-four, both parents are still alive, and the father learned decades after the fact that his ex-wife was back in the country, but I had stranger news for him still.

During the course of my research, I came across some postings by a fellow claiming to be the soldier's son. It was unclear whether the soldier was ever aware of this son, but knowingly or unknowingly, he began a family tradition as both this child and his son (named after the soldier) went on to join the military. I found the professed son and grandson serving in Iraq and South Korea, respectively.

The resolution at this juncture remains unknown. I made the decision to inform the German relatives (through a diplomatic, native-born German speaker) of the alleged son and grandson, and to offer contact details if they were wanted. Whether they opt to accept this possibility or do anything about it is their choice. I strongly suspect this is truly the soldier's family, but regardless of my beliefs or preferences, I have to play a neutral, third-party role.

Orphan Chain

Some of the toughest cases are those involving adoption, orphan, or foster care situations. I recall one that was doubly difficult because the soldier was a Swedish immigrant, and when I traced him back across the pond, I learned that he had been raised in foster care. Due to the thoroughness and accessibility of Swedish records, his family was found, but I'm not always as lucky in America.

Some of you might think the heading of this section is a typo and that I meant orphan *train*, but this is actually deliberate—though the so-called orphan train was involved. If you're not familiar with it, the orphan train movement involved the transfer of perhaps 200,000 orphaned, abandoned, and homeless children, primarily from New York City to rural areas. All told, forty-seven states and Canada were involved.

Every once in a while, my cases include one of these children, though it's usually not the soldier himself. In fact, it's almost always his mother. When this happens, it's often possible to solve it due to assistance from the New York Foundling Hospital, which handled many of these adoptions and retained good records, but one family stands out in my memory because I eventually learned that the soldier's mother was a third-generation orphan.

I determined that his mother had lost her parents, but was able to learn their names through the Foundling—only to follow her mother's trail (looking for relatives with the same mtDNA) and ascertain that she was also an orphan. Imagine my frustration when I finally succeeded in identifying the soldier's grandmother's family and then learned that *her* mother—the soldier's great-grandmother—had also been orphaned.

Regretfully, this remains one of my unsolved cases because the great-grandmother was an immigrant from Ireland with a common name. Given the time frame, it simply wasn't possible to pursue the family any further back in time, and due to the chain of lost parents, the family was lean with no other mtDNA prospects. But the good news is that science is now coming to the rescue. Since the time of this research, Y-DNA (using samples contributed by paternal relatives) has become an alternative, and this is exactly the exceptional kind of case that warrants its use.

No More mtDNA

Dwelling a bit more on mtDNA, I should mention that it's possible but very rare for it to essentially die out in a family. If a soldier was an only child, for instance, you can go back to his mother. If she's passed away, you can search for any sisters she had or their children. If, say, she only had brothers, then you can go back to her mother, the soldier's grandmother, and repeat the process. Each time you run out of mtDNA candidates in a given generation, you back up another one, find fresh contenders, and then trace their lines forward to their living descendants.

In most cases, this process will net you some appropriate maternal relatives within a few generations, but a select few families resist resolution. Sometimes waltzing back to great-grandma means that you're now dealing with another country, which can inject another layer of complexity. And each time you back up, you've got more time to travel back across to get to the present and find living cousins—not to mention the sheer number of candidates who may need to be researched.

Once in a great while, I'll march back a century or two and track countless cousins' lines, only to have them peter out. I'll find myself at my keyboard sighing as I discover that this one became a nun, this one died young, and this one only had sons—the last of whom died in 2006. The most extreme example was a Vietnam soldier whose family had done such a spectacular job of shedding mtDNA kin that I ultimately found it necessary to reverse all the way back to 1700 before finding a viable branch that made it all the way back to the twenty-first century.

Of course, the natural corollary of reaching so far afield in the soldier's family tree is the experience of cold-calling his third cousins once removed. It tends to make for an interesting conversation when you contact a stranger to discuss a relative they've never heard of who lost his life in WWII. Oddly, this has become a rather normal chat for me, and I remain grateful for the many wonderful souls who have checked the urge to hang up on me, and have instead, heard me out. I think it speaks volumes that the vast majority I call ultimately agree to provide DNA samples, if requested.

"The Number You Have Called..."

"The number you have called has been disconnected or is no longer in service." I don't even want to think about how many times this annoying recording has derailed my quest to reach a soldier's family. As I mentioned earlier, the United States is a ridiculously mobile society. Over the last few decades, we've become a nation of vagabonds, chasing this dream, warmer weather, that boyfriend, lower taxes, or that job. Whatever the impetus, Americans are constantly on the move.

Over recent years we've also become far more obsessed with privacy, as well as much more jaded and suspicious. Over a third of us are hiding behind unlisted numbers, a figure that's soaring due to many dropping traditional landlines. Sad to say, the poor economy means that many of us are running from creditors, and use blocking tools to prevent them from reaching us. And if someone does manage to penetrate all the filters we've set up to make ourselves hard to reach, we're on our guard. Still, I'm grateful for the chance to communicate with relatives, even if they're wary. I can cope with the "Why should I believe you?" and "How do I know this isn't a scam?" concerns if I can at least reach them.

The last decade has developed into something of an accidental social experiment for me since I've been consistently cold calling families all this time. I've been a front-row witness to all these changes, and frankly, my work has become more difficult because of it. It's beyond frustrating to execute some clever research to find a family, only to not be able to talk with them, but it happens all the time. So what do I do when the usual avenues of contact don't work? I get creative!

I'm not proud. I'll do whatever works. Funeral home directors and small town librarians are some of my best friends. If it's still in business, I'll call the funeral parlor that handled the soldier's mother's service in 1996, and see if they can direct me to other family members. Librarians in rural areas will often steer me to older local residents or the town historian.

Was a church mentioned in the obituary of a relative? You can be sure I'm going to call it. Did a human interest story in the local newspaper mention a cousin who worked at this restaurant or that hairdresser? They're next on my list for a chat. I've called neighbors, asking if they'll pop a note in the mailbox for me, and in a pinch, I might even call the police or fire department to ask them to play middleman (for emergency purposes, they usually have current phone numbers, even if unlisted) with a family I'm trying to reach.

I made contact with the homeless brother of one soldier by calling a mall that a police report indicated he frequented. Apparently he lived in the woods behind the Family Dollar store. Another useful tactic? Deliberately calling others with the same name in the same town. In one case, this led to a conversation with a woman who knew exactly who I meant since she and the other woman both had Chihuahuas and the vet was always getting their records mixed up. You better believe my next call was to that veterinarian.

And then, of course, there's the wear-out-the-phone approach. When I'm reasonably certain that I have the right number, but no one ever answers, I'll call over and over. Sooner or later, curiosity tends to win out and someone picks up the phone. In one instance, a family finally called me after numerous attempts on my part to reach them. They cheerfully admitted to hearing my name repeatedly on their answering machine, but thought I was a bill collector. What changed? They went shopping and happened to see my name and photo on a box of family history software, and realized I was telling the truth. Dumb luck on my part, but it did the job!

The Quest Continues

So I continue to cope with all that these cases dish out—the mother who married so many times that I had to follow her through half a dozen surnames, the parents who gave several of their children the same name (George Foreman was not the first!), and even the mother who split her twin sons between her first and second husbands (the surviving eighty-three-year-old son's children didn't believe his claim of being a twin until I called). I research my way past name changes and track down the relatives no one's seen since the 1970s. In short, I rack my brain for ways to get around whatever brick walls might spring up that could potentially block me from finding a soldier's relatives and contribute to his eventual identification. Each time I succeed, I become a better detective. And occasionally, I get the privilege of attending the long overdue funeral of a hero.

Not long ago, I had the opportunity to attend the burial ceremony for Thomas D. Costello at Arlington National Cemetery. Thomas was one of "my boys," an Irish-born soldier who gave his life for his adopted country on the battlefields of France in 1918. In a spooky coincidence, I was about to go on vacation to Ireland almost exactly where he was originally from, so I was able to walk the streets of his youth and tell those in his hometown of his heroism. On another occasion, I was the only one to attend the funeral for a soldier who lost his life in Korea, so I had the honor of receiving the flag on behalf of the family (later sent to them, of course). The memory of that moment is all it takes to reinvigorate me whenever I confront the inevitable challenges my work entails. After all, what I deal with pales in comparison to the sacrifices of these brave and noble soldiers.

CHAPTER TWO

Famous Cousins

*Barack Obama and Sarah Palin
are related—*Yawn**

YOU'VE SEEN THE HEADLINES. Barack Obama and Sarah Palin are cousins! Madonna and Ellen DeGeneres are cousins! Britney Spears and John Edwards are cousins! Whoa, what do you know? Obama is also cousins with Dick Cheney, Brad Pitt, George Bush, Harry Truman, Warren Buffett, and Rush Limbaugh! What are the odds? Oh, about 100 percent.

Well, maybe not 100 percent. I should probably refrain from addressing one form of hyperbole with another, so I'll temper my last statement and reduce the odds to 95 percent. And in the interest of full disclosure, I have to confess that I'm also guilty of participation. The Obama-Pitt (ninth cousins) and Edwards-Spears (seventh cousins, three times removed) connections are both my doing, so I haven't exactly been an innocent bystander in the "I can't believe they're related" game. But I'm over it, and I hope everyone else is too.

Here's why: if you go back far enough, we're all cousins. Granted, the relationships that link many of us exist back in pre-documented times, so many genuine cousinships will never be known. But mathematically, we all have millions of cousins.

Keeping It in the Family

Think about it. You have two parents, four grandparents, eight great-grandparents, and so on. Skip back through ten generations and you have 1,024 direct line ancestors. Notice that I said "direct line." That means we're not even considering siblings or cousins—just those specific great-great-greats who contributed to your gene pool. March back another ten generations and you have over a million direct ancestors. If you continue traveling back in time, you won't have much further to go until reaching the point where the number of your ancestors seemingly exceeds the world's population at that time. But how can that be?

In genealogical terms, the answer is pedigree collapse, but most know the phenomenon as kissing cousins. Many enjoy taking jabs at West Virginia and royal families for their alleged, excessive inbreeding, but the reality is that all our family trees are littered with kissing cousins.

Even a mere two hundred years ago (a blip in the history of mankind), very few of our forebears lived in cities. Transportation opportunities were also minimal, so when it came time to marry, your prospects were limited to a small supply of candidates who lived nearby. Barring some major upheaval such as war or famine, those nearby probably descended from people who had lived in that vicinity for countless generations. And so did you. Result? Knowingly or unknowingly, you married your cousin.

Evidence of this can be seen in church records of the last few centuries. It's not unusual to see dispensations for cousin marriages adorning perhaps every ninth or tenth marriage, but those were just for the known relationships. If they had had family tree software back in the 1700s, it would have been the rare marriage that didn't sport a dispensation.

Cousins who marry cousins have overlapping ancestors. If they're second cousins, for instance, they share a pair of great-grandparents, as well as all the ancestors of that couple. Removing those duplicate ancestors from the family tree means that descendants of the kissing cousins will have far fewer *unique* ancestors. The size of the overall family tree therefore shrinks significantly—hence the term "pedigree collapse."

That's before we factor in quirks we've conveniently forgotten such as the habit of many of our ancestors of marrying siblings of a deceased spouse. Back in the not-so-distant days when women routinely died in childbirth, it was not unusual for a fellow to go through three or four wives. Rapid remarriage was the norm and single sisters of the deceased wife were often convenient contenders since they frequently stepped in—and actually moved in—to help with the children. It was a solution that worked for everyone.

Nor was this gender-specific. In many cultures, if the husband died, his wife would marry one of his brothers—typically a younger one. Though driven by economic necessity rather than a desire for eye-candy escorts, many of our great-great-great-grandmothers would qualify in today's terms as "cougars."

The most extreme example I've seen of keeping it in the family was a trio of marriages that occurred on the same day. It was one thing that a pair of brothers married a pair of sisters—that wasn't all that uncommon. But the widowed parents of the assorted, younger brides and grooms also married each other that day. Who knows how many pedigrees collapsed upon themselves due to that single marital escapade?

Famous Cousin Sweet Spot

The same protection-of-the-clan mentality that led to marriages with close kin also contributed to large families. How many children would it take to keep the farm going and how many would die young? Hard to say, so better have lots of children.

Take that same math discussed earlier and reverse the flow. Let's say that a pair of your eighth great-grandparents had five children who survived to adulthood and had their own children (a conservative assumption). Reproducing at the same rate, the ensuing generations would give that couple 25 grandchildren, 125 great-grandchildren, 625 great-great-grandchildren, and so forth. Even allowing for a considerable easing of the birth rate in recent generations, you would be one of millions of their descendants. And all of this is within a genealogically relevant time frame, meaning recent enough that the generations may well be traceable on paper. If we estimate three generations per century (again, a reasonable assumption), this couple would have lived in perhaps the late 1600s, so we're dealing with a typical colonial family.

Now rewind North American history to those colonial days. There weren't many of European origin here at the time, but those who were here were mostly living in rural areas, accidentally or otherwise marrying cousins, and having large families with children who repeated the pattern. In many places, this pattern wasn't disturbed until sometime in the twentieth century. Come forward three or four centuries from this initial couple and it is inevitable that their descendants will be hopelessly interrelated. And a few of those descendants, for whatever reasons, will become famous.

Colonial times in North America constitute a famous cousin sweet spot. They're long enough ago that genealogical math has had a chance to work its magic, but recent enough that there's often a paper trail to follow. That's why—if you pay attention the next time you hear a famous cousin revelation—the touted connections almost always involve a shared colonial American or French-Canadian (our pilgrim contemporaries) ancestor. And the living celebrities will rarely be more closely related than seventh cousins. In fact, they're most often eighth, ninth, or tenth cousins. About the only exceptions to this pattern are those who are related even more distantly, generally through a royal ancestor who lived back before America and Canada existed.

Finding the Famous

This reality explains why Barack Obama is such a popular subject for famous cousin revelations. While his father was from Kenya, his mother has deep American roots that meander back to the early days of Maryland, Virginia, and Massachusetts (not to mention New Jersey, Pennsylvania, Kentucky, Ohio, Tennessee, Arkansas, Illinois, Missouri, Indiana, West Virginia, Oklahoma, and Kansas). I'm probably missing a few states, but the point is that his family is well-represented in colonial America.

For this reason, a hefty percentage of all Americans are somehow related to Obama, so it doesn't impress me that he has a smattering of famous cousins. Of course he does. What impresses me more is that someone took the time to ferret out any given connection. It's not particularly clever to find someone's famous cousins, but it can be time-consuming. How exactly do you pluck, say, Palin out of Obama's millions of cousins? The process generally starts by familiarizing yourself with the target's family tree. The most direct way to do this is to simply research it, as I did with then-candidate Obama in 2007.

From there, it's a matter of browsing books and other resources looking for similar names, or at least, locations. It doesn't hurt that families of early arrivers have been extensively scrutinized, allowing genealogists to get a running start by skimming through compilations of *Mayflower* descendants, presidential families, and the like. In recent years, celebrity genealogy has become something of a sub-hobby, so it's sometimes possible to surf your way to speculative connections, or increasingly, tap into master databases designed to facilitate the discovery of famous cousins.

Once you find the name of a possible shared ancestor, you might think that the work is done, but this is where the effort truly begins. Many of those same resources that can provide a jump start are riddled with errors. One popular, online tool for finding famous cousins, for example, does an excellent job of leading researchers astray by incorporating entertaining details such as women giving birth at age seventy or an immigrant couple in the 1700s having twelve children in Massachusetts, only to inexplicably return to England to have their thirteenth. That's because these tools, while potentially helpful, still aren't quite sophisticated enough to consistently sift out poor research or wishful thinking from reality.

One factor frequently used in their algorithms is how many genealogists have included a particular connection in their family trees, but this fails to take into account a troublesome echo-chamber effect. We've already seen that a colonial couple may have millions of descendants today. If one of them makes a mistake and pops it online, it's often not long before some of the other descendants take a shortcut and unwittingly introduce that same error into their own trees. Before long, it looks true because so many are making the same claim, but it's just an inaccuracy repeated many times.

Link by Link

That's why it's necessary to examine every parent-to-child link in both celebrities' family trees to be absolutely sure. And

that's where the genealogical slog fest starts. The first few generations tend to be fairly easy to confirm, but as discussed previously, these links are usually at least eight generations back.
Once you get back to the earliest generations, the paper trail becomes harder and harder to substantiate. A typical famous
cousin connection, then, might involve roughly eighteen or
twenty links, of which four or five might require extensive digging to verify.

Then again, the media doesn't usually ask for proof, but when
I did the Barack Obama–Brad Pitt and Britney Spears–John Edwards projects wearing my Ancestry.com hat, I took the time to
bulletproof the company by methodically delving into every link
in the chain. Incidentally, I happened to make the second connection when Edwards was running for president and just as
Britney was having a bit of a meltdown, shaving her head and
otherwise confounding the rest of us. It would have been easy to
attract attention by joining the media circus at the time, so I remain grateful to the CEO for taking the high road and waiting
until Britney's life had settled down.

Truthfully, some of the most tedious research I've ever done
has involved famous cousins. That's because you're not really
discovering anything new. What you're mostly doing is an initial
scoping of possibilities, followed by painstaking verification of
assertions made by others in the past. Forget the thrill of the
hunt so often associated with genealogical sleuthing; this is just
following someone else's well-worn trail and hoping that they
didn't take a wrong turn.

The upside is that with experience—and databases slowly im-
proving—it gets easier to spot fresh possibilities. With Hillary
Clinton, for instance, seven of her eight great-grandparents were
immigrants, but that last branch is French-Canadian—which is
why we've been treated to stories about her being related to
Madonna, Angelina, Celine, and Shania (which, in turn, leads
me to muse what it is about French-Canadian heritage that
spawns women of enough prominence to be known primarily by

their first names). Find even one French-Canadian ancestor in a celebrity's family tree, and it's a good bet that you'll eventually be able to link her (with the exception of Ricky Gervais, it is almost always a female) to other notables of the same heritage (welcome to the party, Avril Lavigne and Alanis Morissette!). This is primarily due to particularly large family sizes (remember, Celine Dion is the youngest of fourteen), which amplifies the cousinship effect.

With a bit of practice, you also get better at noticing gateway ancestors—that is, a person who lived a few centuries ago who is already known to have quite a few famous descendants. Immigrant Mareen Duvall comes to mind. He's the common link among Obama, Cheney, Buffett, and Truman, so if the family tree of the president elected in 2020 leads back to Duvall, the headline is already written.

Genetic Cousins

A recent variation on the famous cousin theme is a proliferation of claims of genetically discovered connections. Ozzy Osbourne and Stephen Colbert are cousins? Eva Longoria and Yo-Yo Ma are cousins? Well, kind of.

They're cousins in the sense that you and I are probably cousins. Perhaps they have the same maternal haplogroup, or branch of the world's family tree, which means that they share a female ancestor who lived, oh, sometime around 10,000 to 45,000 years ago. Maybe it's on a paternal branch. Or perhaps they have a few brief, overlapping chromosomal segments that hint of a common ancestor in the distant past.

Don't get me wrong. I'm a longtime proponent of genetic genealogy, and it offers a genuine means to uncover unexpected or long-sought connections, as we've seen from a growing number of adoption search success stories (as well as at least one savvy teenager who used it to help identify his sperm donor). It's also an approach that will become more powerful over time as more and more people join in. The more of us who take ancestrally oriented DNA tests, the better the odds for everyone of finding new cousins. But so far, none of the genetic, famous cousin tales that has attracted attention has concerned a connection that could confidently be said to exist within the last thousand years. It will happen. It just hasn't yet.

The Cousin Litmus Test

If your family includes even a single branch of early European arrivers to North America, your odds of having oodles of documentable cousins with a few famous ones sprinkled in the mix are very high. And finding them is becoming easier all the time. So the next time you hear that celebrity A and celebrity B are cousins, ask yourself two questions:

1. Are they more closely related than seventh cousins?
2. Was the common ancestor *not* a colonial American, French-Canadian, or royal?

If the answer to both of these questions is yes, then you're dealing with a tweet-worthy announcement you might want to share with others. But if the answer is no, in the words of intensively cousined Shania Twain, "that don't impress me much."

CHAPTER THREE

Serial Centenarians

*Could two relatives who knew each other
live in four centuries?*

I SUPPOSE I SHOULD start out by 'fessing up that I came up a little
shy in terms of complete resolution on the following case, but
this was a challenge I couldn't resist. After all, how could I *not* be
intrigued by a query like this?

> We would like to find out if there is anyone still alive in
> America who met a relative that was born in the 18th
> century. We figure this would take someone who is at
> least 100 years old, and who had an ancestor who lived
> to be more than 100. Hypothetically, it could be someone
> who was born in 1901 and who that year met their
> great-grandmother, who was born in 1799.

This request came, as many of mine do, from a media outlet.
For reasons I'll get into shortly, they opted not to share what I
eventually pieced together, but I contend that it's still slightly
amazing and deserves an airing, so here goes.

Is It Possible?

Was it even worth contemplating? Was there any chance that there was anyone out there who fit the bill? I debated at length whether I should fend off the urge to take on such a daunting case or allow myself to give in to temptation.

I caved.

As I considered the odds, I recalled writing several years ago about the grandsons of President John Tyler, born in 1790, who were still very much alive. This was due to remarkably long generations. President Tyler fathered a child when he was about sixty-three, and this child had a son when he was about seventy-five. The result was generation spans about three times the norm— or almost seventy years per generation. To be sure, this was impressive, but the twentieth-century grandsons never came close to meeting their eighteenth-century-born grandfather. In fact, they didn't enter the stage until more than half a century after their presidential forebear had exited.

Could I possibly find a family where any two generations— *whose lives had overlapped*—could claim a reach of four centuries? I honestly didn't know, but I was curious to find out.

Searching for Centenarians

Since this case was a little out of the ordinary, I had to put some thought into how to approach it. How would I even begin? Common sense suggested that it would be wiser to find centenarians around 1900 and look for their descendants, rather than find present-day centenarians and hope to "luck into" one who had known—if only briefly—an equally long-lived ancestor. I figured the earlier centenarians were a rarer breed, so I should start with them.

So I knew what my first objective was, but how would I find such people? After some noodling, I brainstormed two ways to develop a short list of candidate families to investigate in greater depth, and both of them centered on database diving.

First, I went to Ancestry.com, home to more than six billion genealogical records. I selected an underused portion of the website that houses the company's historical newspaper collection. Here I entered "centenarian" in the keyword field, and limited the search to 1900–1905. My hope was to bubble up articles that mentioned members of the 100-plus crowd at that time. Even today, we frequently encounter articles about this or that centenarian celebrating his 103rd birthday, recounting how he came to America through Ellis Island in 1921 or likes to regale his family with stories about his first encounter with a car. Surely, I calculated, living so long would have been even more newsworthy back then.

All told, I found over 500 articles. Because there were so many, I spot-checked a number of them, but paid extra attention to obituaries in a database of major metropolitan newspapers. I reasoned that any candidates that cropped up here had probably generated a little buzz and might be easier to trace. Plenty of obituaries and other helpful articles profiling a number of centenarians across the United States emerged.

Then I took another approach. I surfed my way to a database of the 1900 U.S. Federal Census (found on several websites), which lists everyone living in America at the time, and searched for people born in the 1790s (1795, ± 5 years). I repeated the search a couple of times, restricting it to individuals who were related to the head of their household as a grandmother or grandfather. My goal in applying this particular limitation was popping up folks who were living with at least two other generations of their family. In other words, I was hoping to make the rest of the search easier by finding candidates residing with related toddlers who, with a bit of luck, would eventually make it past the century mark themselves and still be kicking it today. If so, it would be clear that they had met their centenarian ancestor since they had lived together.

Finding the Fakers

So now I had two preliminary and overlapping lists of target prospects. The next step was to prune and combine the two, removing duplicates and eliminating those with no readily apparent family connections. But then I needed to do some serious weeding.

It pained me, but I knew that I had to screen out the imposters. How many of these folks, I wondered, were really as old as they claimed? Today, aging is regarded as something to be avoided at all costs, but in a time of sky-high mortality rates, being elderly gave you bragging rights. It meant you were a survivor and that was something to be proud of. Just as someone today might knock a few years off if asked about their age, our ancestors did the reverse and padded the true figure. Being a lifelong genealogist, I knew the pattern well: back in the day, the older you got, the *older* you got.

Knowing what was ahead, I braced myself and started investigating the names from the combined list by searching for them one at a time in earlier census records. The 1890 census had mostly been destroyed (fire and water damage), but I backtracked through the 1880, 1870, and 1860 census records, plucking out the alleged centenarians at earlier stages in their lives. Time and time again, the person who claimed to be 100+ in the 1900 census turned out to really have been born in, say, 1810. Just as I had expected, there was a lot of exaggerating going on. And why not? If you were ninety or so back when there were few formal birth records, why shouldn't you embellish and tack on a few extra years? Heck, making it to ninety was a big accomplishment. You deserved a little attention, didn't you? So why not round up? And round up they did.

The 1799/1800 Debate

With all the names I was forced to scratch off, my list became considerably shorter. I was eventually left with only a dozen or so possibilities, so now it was time to start researching their toddler housemates. Naturally, I was most drawn to households with lots of kids, and one especially appealed to me.

A fellow by the name of Hiram Cronk had been born in April 1800. At least I think he was born in April 1800. In every single census and other record I found, he was listed as having been born in April of either 1799 or 1800. And he lived until 1905, so Hiram was definitely a contender. Or so I thought.

This is where the media organization and I went our separate ways. They maintained that it only counted if he had been born in 1799, but I responded that though 1799 would have admittedly been a touch more exciting, 1800 was still technically part of the eighteenth century. Besides, I pointed out, he was born in the month of April, so he had at least been *conceived* in the 1700s. But they weren't having it. I hesitated briefly and marched on. I was simply too curious to stop.

What made Hiram even more interesting was the fact that he had been the last survivor of the War of 1812. He had joined up with his father and older brother when just a youngster, so was a novelty and a bit of a celebrity in his last few years. I found colorful articles that related how he still received marriage proposals from women who hoped to become his widow and receive his generous pension (between the State of New York and the U.S. Government, almost $100 a month—a lot of money in the early 1900s). I also enjoyed his claims of downing two gallons of wine every month, and was stunned to find footage of his 1905 funeral on the Library of Congress website.

I couldn't help it. I was smitten with Hiram.

Hiram's Progeny

Now my attention shifted to the children associated with Hiram. There were three youngsters living with him in 1900— his great-grandchildren, Mattie, Milo, and James. But knowing that he had lived until 1905, I jumped forward to the 1910 census for this family and picked up more children, three of whom had been born between 1900 and 1905. So now I had a total of six children—the earlier three, and Wayne, Jane, and Donald—who had lived with Hiram.

I set about trying to find these half dozen children, and much to my disappointment—though not surprise—I found the deaths of all of them. Except Jane. Jane was born around 1902 and was now my only hope, but I couldn't find her. Had she lived? If so, had she married and into what name? I looked for obituaries for her siblings that might have mentioned Jane under her married name, but no luck. This was a seemingly obituary-less family. I realized the odds were stacked against her having lived more than 100 years, and was on the verge of moving on to another candidate, but then I caught a minor break.

Jane-Hunting

In the 1930 census for this same family, I spotted Jane living at home with the rest of them. But then I did a double take. Jane was listed as Janet, and was younger than expected. In fact, a lot younger. Was this a transcription error? No, I inspected the image, and "Janet" was fifteen, so born around 1915—not 1902 like Jane. So this was a different daughter. For whatever reasons, the parents had given two daughters very similar names.

I backed up to the 1920 census, and sure enough, there were both Jane M. and Jeannette H. Cronk. So this meant that Jane was no longer with her family in 1930. What had happened to her?

By 1920, the family was living in Rochester, New York, so I did one of my "nothing to lose" searches. Jane is a common name, but I went to the 1930 census and looked for any Janes living in Rochester who had been born in 1902 (± 2 years, to add a little wiggle room in case her age was slightly off). I sighed as a total of forty-one possibilities popped up. Just as I feared, too many prospects to spot my target. But then I noticed that only one had the middle initial of M. Of course, most of them simply hadn't included their middle initial, but still. Maybe it was worth a shot.

Oh No

What happened next took the wind out of my sails. The Jane M. I found in the 1930 census had married into a distinctive Dutch name, making her easier to trace forward in time. While I appreciated that the chances were that she had passed away, I held on to hope that I wouldn't find her in our national death index. But there she was. I was crushed to learn that she had died in 2003.

Wait! 2003. True, she was no longer with us, but if this was the right Jane, she had lived to the age of 101. Her great-grandfather had lived from 1800 to 1905, she had lived from 1902 to 2003, and they had overlapped lives in the same house from 1902 to 1905. Pretty impressive, even if she wasn't alive. But how could I find out whether this was really the right Jane? After all, I had selected this one just because of her middle initial. I needed proof.

Since she had only passed away a few years ago, I did some digging in a few people-finding websites that provide addresses for living people. Typically, folks take a decade or so after passing away to fade from these databases, so it wasn't that unusual to find her. At one of her addresses, I noticed another resident who appeared to be her daughter—a woman with the same first name and age of her young daughter from the 1930 census. And then I spotted another name associated with the residence— Cronk. A Cronk had lived there once upon a time. This almost had to be the right family.

It was 8:00 on a Saturday evening. Not that there's ever a good time to cold-call a stranger with a peculiar quest like this, but I picked up the phone and called the possible daughter. It took a few minutes for her to warm up to me, but by the end of the conversation, we were buddies. Yes, Jane Cronk was indeed her mother, and yes, she knew all about her great-great-grandfather, Hiram Cronk. And oh, by the way, did I know that her grandmother had shot a stranger through the front door? I hadn't until that moment, but this new tidbit simply reinforced my long-held belief that there's no such thing as a boring family!

Pretty Close

As I mentioned at the outset, I came up a little shy. I didn't find a living person who fit the bill, but Hiram and Jane met the other specifications. Between the two of them, they had lived 1800–2003—the whole of the nineteenth and twentieth centuries with a dash of the bookend eighteenth and twenty-first centuries.

That pile of dates might not sound all that remarkable, but to put this in perspective, consider that they jointly lived through every U.S. president except George Washington and Barack Obama. Still not impressed? I recently shared this story with an audience in New Zealand, and realized that American presidents were a less than ideal reference point, so instead, came up with another way to help them grasp the time frame involved. Between the two of them, Hiram and Jane lived through all of the following:

- Napoleonic Wars
- Slavery abolished in British Empire
- Charles Darwin's theory of evolution
- Potato famine in Ireland
- Civil War and end of slavery in United States
- Unification of Germany and Italy

- Russian Revolution
- WWI and WWII
- North and South Poles explored
- Women's suffrage
- The Great Depression
- Man on the moon
- Fall of communism in Europe and end of apartheid in South Africa
- Inventions of gaslight, steam engine, sewing machine, telephone, lightbulb, cars, airplanes, radio, TV, polio vaccine, satellite, PC, Internet
- Opening of Chunnel and intro of Euro
- Sequencing of human genome

The media outlet that had prompted this investigation refused to declare victory, but I did. Perhaps there's another family with someone still living, and if so, I'd be delighted to learn about them. But for now, I think it's a kick to have discovered Hiram and Jane, great-grandfather and great-granddaughter, and serial centenarians.

CHAPTER FOUR

Alex Haley Was Scottish?

Uncovering the unexpected heritage of
Roots *author, Alex Haley, through DNA*

ONE OF THE MORE memorable experiences I've had in my genealogical career was having a front-row seat to an extraordinary reunion brought about through DNA. In fact, I was largely responsible for it. Though many are still learning of it, genetic testing for the purpose of peering into one's ancestral past has been around for a decade, but few would have expected it to reveal that the Haley family—as in that of Alex Haley—was Scottish.

If you've been doing genealogy for even twenty minutes (and probably even if you haven't yet dabbled), you know that Alex Haley wrote *Roots*, which led to a massively popular miniseries. Decades later, the series still remains one of America's most-watched shows. The book and series jointly brought millions into the world of genealogy back in the 1970s and since. You may well be one of those millions.

Rooted in *Roots*

Roots focused on the maternal side of Alex Haley's family tree, but he also wrote *Queen* about his father's side. Queen was Alex Haley's paternal grandmother (movie buffs might recall that she was portrayed by a then young unknown named Halle Berry), and was married to Alec Haley.

Alec died back in 1918, and sadly, as was so often the case for a person born into slavery, his death certificate simply said "don't know" for the names of his parents. This is just one of the many frustrating challenges that often confront African American researchers, but family lore can occasionally keep alive information that is not to be found in official records. Such was the case with the Haleys.

In *Queen*, Alex Haley discusses his namesake grandfather, stating, "Alec had taken the name Haley from his true Massa, although his real father's name was Baugh." He goes on to say that Baugh was an overseer at the Haley plantation in Marion County, Alabama. This is the story that had been carefully shepherded to Alex by his father.

A little poking around in records of that time and place quickly turns up slave-owning Haleys in Marion County, but no conspicuous candidates for Baugh. And while there were some Baughs in neighboring counties, none of them were clear contenders for Alec's father, making it difficult to verify the family tale. So it remained just that—a story passed down through the generations.

Origins of a Genetic Reunion

This is where DNA enters the picture. I have the good fortune of being friends with Chris Haley, a nephew of Alex's. Chris is an archivist with the State of Maryland and an amateur genealogist himself, and our paths had crossed at a family reunion conference some years back.

In 2007, I invited Chris to attend the Federation of Genealogical Societies' annual conference on behalf of Roots Television, an online channel of family history videos I had launched the previous year. I thought it would be both fun and appropriate to have him there to represent the Haley family on the thirtieth anniversary of *Roots*.

As it happened, it was at this conference that Ancestry.com entered the genetic genealogy market. Though I was Ancestry's chief family historian at the time, I didn't know the company had chosen that moment to introduce its first DNA testing kits, but as soon as I learned, I instantly thought of Chris. How amazing would it be to see what could be detected genetically about the Haley family?

I dashed back to my booth and asked Chris if he'd be game to get tested. Happily, he humored me and agreed. Better yet, wearing my Roots Television hat, I had a camera crew at the event, and he was kind enough to consent to be filmed as he took his test. I sometimes share the video in my genetic genealogy talks because Chris manages to makes swabbing the inside of his cheek entertaining—which gives you an idea what a lively personality he has!

Why the Y Test?

The test that Chris took was the most popular kind—Y-DNA. Only males have a Y-chromosome and it's passed intact down through the generations. This is wildly convenient for genealogists because this is the same way that surnames get passed down in most cultures, so the Y-DNA and surnames travel in tandem through time.

In the case of the Haley family, if the oral tradition was true, Chris would have inherited his Y-DNA from his father, Julius (Alex's brother), who would have inherited from his father, Simon, who would have inherited from his father, Alec, who would have inherited it from the white overseer named Baugh. In short, as a direct line male descendant, Chris is a living representative of this alleged Baugh.

The Waiting Game

When Chris's results came, he learned that the Haley branch of his family is haplogroup R1b. I like to think of haplogroups as branches of a massive family tree of mankind. Your haplogroup is the branch that your family comes from, and R1b meant that the progenitor of this line was definitely European—and odds are, of British Isles stock. While this certainly supported the family story, it fell well shy of confirming it.

Chris also had a genetic mate in the database—someone whose paternal genetic signature matched his exactly, indicating a common ancestor. Normally, this is an exciting prospect, but rather frustratingly, this person was listed as anonymous. Even after Chris attempted to communicate via the blind e-mail service provided, he chose to remain under wraps. This is fairly unusual as the main reason to take a Y-DNA test is to find people who match you—your genetic cousins. But some have other interests or objectives, so occasionally, you can encounter someone who doesn't want to compare notes to see where your family trees might converge.

At this point, Chris experienced an opportunity to practice the art of patience. His results sat in the database while he waited...and waited...and waited. Then finally—about eighteen months after he tested—he received notification of another match. Fortunately, this person had not chosen to remain anonymous, and a map showed that he lived in the British Isles. But the real eye-opener was this fellow's name—Thomas Baff!

Baff is just another spelling of Baugh (think of "laugh" with a "b"), so this was an aha moment worth waiting for. Alex Haley claimed their ancestor was a white man named Baugh, and out of all the people in the world who had DNA tested, Chris matched a man named Baff. The family lore was true.

Genetic Courtship

Chris was excited but apprehensive about finding this new match. Making that initial contact with a genetic cousin can give you a feeling not unlike first-date jitters. Mr. Anonymous hadn't been interested in communicating. Would Chris be rejected again? He used the e-mail brokerage system and sent off a message to Thomas Baff.

Thomas turned out to be June Baff Black, Thomas's daughter—and much to Chris's delight, she responded. In fact, she was thrilled to be contacted! June's parents had done a fair bit of genealogical research back in the 1980s, but she was new to it herself, having only started researching three weeks prior to hearing from Chris.

Several months earlier, she had watched an episode of the U.K. version of *Who Do You Think You Are?* that involved the DNA testing of a popular British athlete. June was fascinated, so her husband suggested that she ask for a test for Christmas, which is exactly what she did. Since women don't have a Y-chromosome, she nudged her father to swab his cheek while visiting during the holidays, and then promptly sent off the kit.

E-mails flew back and forth across the Atlantic with Chris in Maryland and June living in Wales, though Scottish through and through. Thanks to her parents' earlier research, June already knew the Baugh line back to the 1760s, and all this time, her family had stayed in the same area—West Lothian. The new-found cousins took the time to get to know each other and learned of a shared passion for the performing arts. It seems that more than just a shared Y-DNA signature had been passed down through the generations to both of them!

Next Week in London?

After about a week of exchanges, Chris decided to tell June that he was African American and related to Alex Haley of *Roots* fame. "Decided to tell" might sound like an odd way to put it, but when you start an e-mail–based relationship with a stranger, it's hard to know how they might respond to slightly unexpected information. Chris and I chatted, and I suggested that there was a good chance she already knew since she was web-savvy (an article and video about Chris's DNA test were both online). Just maybe June was waiting until he felt comfortable telling her. We would later learn that I had guessed right, so less than a month into her personal genealogical quest, this genetic virgin found out that she was related to the Haley family.

At this point, everything accelerated. *Who Do You Think You Are Live!*, the largest genealogical event in the world (typically drawing about 15,000 people), was being held the following weekend in London. That seemed the perfect time to meet, especially since the second day was "Scottish Saturday." It was now Sunday. Might it be possible for the cousins to meet on Saturday? I'll be honest with you. This week turned out to be one of the most stressful of my life, but much pleading, persuasion, and persistence—accompanied by frantic rescheduling, rush tickets, and an emergency passport—made it happen. It didn't help that the publicity people who were enlisted to assist were, for reasons I still don't understand, indifferent to the story. In fact, I recall being stunned when one informed me that there would be no interest because "no one knows who Alex Haley is anymore."

BBC Bound

I was already booked to speak at the event, and arrived in London before Chris. After taping a promotional segment to air the following morning on the popular morning show *BBC Breakfast*,

I was asked if I'd be willing to come to the studio the next morning to appear live. I gratefully realized that the perfect opportunity had just presented itself. Sure, I told the producer, I'd be game to come the following morning, but I had something she might like better. In spite of what I had been told about Alex Haley now supposedly being an unknown, the producer took to the Haley-Baff reunion idea instantly.

Chris flew into London that night. The following morning, he and June met for the first time in the hotel lobby where we all were staying. I was amused to see the cousins comparing hands and remarking on assorted similarities, as we all tend to do when meeting distant relatives for the first time. Moments later, they were whisked away to be on *BBC Breakfast* where their reunion would continue on air. After that, the floodgates opened and Chris and June spent the balance of their time in London doing interview after interview.

Cousins Chris Haley and June Baff Black compare hands. (Author)

Only Through DNA

In this case, DNA testing showed that Chris and June are cousins, the Haley family is Scottish in origin, and Alex Haley's oral tradition is true. This last point was particularly important to the Haley family. Many are quick to challenge the veracity of tales that have been passed down through the family, so they were especially pleased that science had supported theirs.

As to when their common ancestor might have lived, that's to be determined. A review of the genealogical and genetic information available at present indicates that this shared ancestor lived roughly between 1600 and 1800, and that Chris and June are probably something in the neighborhood of seventh, eighth, or ninth cousins (and I'm happy to report that they continue to behave like most cousins, keeping in touch via e-mail and Facebook, and getting together once in a while). The paper trail in the relevant time frame is less than ideal, especially on the American side, but it may be possible one day to connect the dots and determine the exact nature of the relationship.

But the very fact that it may not be possible to connect Chris and June through traditional research demonstrates the power of genetic genealogy. Without DNA testing—just a few short years ago—the odds that Chris would ever have been able to discover that he was part Scottish or find his Scottish cousins were slim and none. And there's no chance that June could have possibly learned of her American cousins in a scant three weeks any other way than genetically.

Will Chris be donning a kilt any time soon? If so, I'm sure his cousins would be more than willing to show him how!

CHAPTER FIVE

Egyptian Roots in a Hurry

*Researching Hoda Kotb's roots for
the* Today *show on a fierce deadline*

I'VE APPEARED ON a number of morning and talk shows over the years, and more often than not, wind up delving into the family trees of the hosts. These opportunities tend to crop up rather abruptly, resulting in what might be called roots emergencies. Though many are under the mistaken impression that genealogy is all online and can be done literally overnight, we're nowhere near that family history nirvana. But try telling that to the overworked producer who's juggling dozens of upcoming segments and wants you to appear with the anchor's heritage mapped out by next Tuesday. The last thing she needs is a realities-of-genealogy lecture, so I simply do my best to make it happen.

That's how I've found myself begging someone in Italy to gain entrance to a closed archive over the weekend or racking my brain for ways to investigate a car accident that occurred in the Philippines in the 1940s, preferably within the next forty-eight hours. Because the genealogical gods have been generous with me, I usually pull it off, but even I was apprehensive when asked to appear on the fourth hour of the *Today* show, hosted by Kathie Lee Gifford and Hoda Kotb.

It wasn't Kathie Lee who worried me. I expected her roots to be comparatively easy to trace, and they were. In fact, my concern with her had more to do with episodes of tragedy that laced her family's past. "And then your uncle was killed in World War II" isn't exactly the kind of chitchat that most morning shows welcome, but I felt confident in being able to find plenty to discuss about her roots. It was Hoda who intimidated me.

The Celebrity Handicap

Celebrities are almost always challenging because they're so well-insulated. Even when requested to research a famous individual's ancestry by their own "people," I frequently interact with layers of producers, public-relations professionals, agents, and other buffers designed to keep the well-known from drowning in requests and pleas. I understand all this, but when it comes to genealogy, not being able to chat with your subject is a serious impediment.

In real life, you start your family history by capturing what you already know and then approaching others in the family to add to it. This typically allows you to gather information on two to four generations before hitting the paper trail, but I can't recall a single instance when I've been given access to a celebrity before meeting them—usually on camera for the "reveal" where I share what I've learned. Mind you, I'm not starstruck. I just want to do a good job in a short time, so I'll ask to speak with an aunt or cousin who's into genealogy—or maybe provide a form with some basic questions to be completed. But these requests are generally refused, debated until it's too late, or furnished after I've already pieced things together the hard way.

This, then, is the celebrity handicap. Thanks to privacy laws that protect the living, getting information on that first generation or two can be tricky business. If I'm lucky, I'll be able to google my way to an interview with the celebrity's parents or other family tidbits. But I often wind up burning valuable time trying to learn basics that someone in the family could supply in minutes.

Hoda's Heritage

So it was with Hoda Kotb. As someone with a name others struggle to pronounce, I've always felt a special kinship with people like Hoda whose name induces similar panic. Even the normally unflappable Brian Williams once referred to the eight letters of her name as "the land mine in my teleprompter." Perhaps particularly for this reason, I wanted to be sure that my *Today* show interview was balanced with something for both Hoda and Kathie Lee.

But there was one little problem. Hoda is Oklahoma-born to Egyptian parents. How the heck do you do Egyptian genealogy? I didn't know as I hadn't confronted the need before. And the appearance was scheduled in a week! As sometimes happens, the airing date wound up being pushed off for several weeks (genealogy is rarely breaking news, so I've been bumped for everything from hurricanes to that reality show couple crashing the White House), but I didn't have the luxury of knowing that at the time. As far as I knew, I had to climb Hoda's family tree in the next seven days.

Unfortunately, she hadn't yet published her book (*Hoda: How I Survived War Zones, Bad Hair, Cancer, and Kathie Lee*), which would have provided some useful clues, but the folks at the *Today* show were able to provide one key piece of information to get me started: a great-aunt of hers had been the first female attorney in Egypt. This was just what I needed.

Where Do I Begin?

I sometimes refer to myself as a "recovering management consultant," as that's what I did before becoming a full-time, professional genealogist about a decade ago. Back in my consulting days, I did a lot of globe-trotting—enough that I stopped counting when I reached eighty countries. This means that I know folks in a lot of places, so not knowing what else to do, I decided to tap into that network.

I reached out to an old friend, Saro Nakashian, who lives in the Armenian Quarter of the Old City in Jerusalem. Saro's not a genealogist, but he's one of those fellows who's good at troubleshooting and dreaming up solutions. Jerusalem isn't in Egypt, of course, but all the Egyptians I know live in the United States, so I decided I'd try contacting someone who was more or less in the neighborhood.

To be Armenian is to live in a diaspora situation. If you're of Armenian heritage, you probably have cousins in Los Angeles, Paris, and somewhere in the Middle East. Saro is no exception. I explained my situation and he immediately offered to call a cousin who lived in Cairo. Perfect!

Saro shared all that I had told him, and his cousin kindly agreed to do a little digging for me. But she was also a busy woman with lots of responsibilities and pressing deadlines, so she couldn't give the effort too much time. What she opted to do was some Arabic-language googling to find information about Hoda's great-aunt, the lawyer. The good news is that she found two articles; the bad news is that they were in Arabic.

I wasn't about to reward her generosity by asking for translations, so now I had to think through what to do with links for a pair of articles that just might include some insight into Hoda's family.

An American Cousin in Poland

Brainstorming how to get these articles translated, I thought of my distant cousin, Thom Kolton. Thom and I met in the late 1990s through a village association. All the Smolenyaks in the world come from a village called Osturna that's located in present-day Slovakia. It's one of those tiny towns where everyone is ultimately related to everyone else, so once I started a Smolenyak family newsletter, it quickly morphed into a village-based newsletter. This led to a chain of events that culminated in a village reunion in 1996. Forty Americans whose parents, grandparents, and great-grandparents had come from Osturna traveled there to meet their old country cousins. I thought it was a once-in-a-lifetime experience, but I was wrong.

In 1998, to accommodate those who weren't able to come to Osturna, I decided to organize another reunion, but this time in Pennsylvania. Unbeknownst to me, a petition was circulated at this second reunion saying essentially, "We want to go back to Slovakia." While I was also nostalgic for Osturna and eager to return myself, I didn't have the time to orchestrate another overseas adventure for several dozen Americans. Never dreaming that anyone would step up to the plate, I issued an appeal in the next newsletter for someone to arrange the next reunion. Thom, who was new to our community at the time, immediately offered to do just that.

Thom's the kind of guy who doesn't do things halfway. I learned this when he moved from Baltimore to Slovakia to learn Slovak and set up the next reunion. Now *that's* commitment. Thom had subsequently returned to the United States, but found that he liked Eastern Europe so much that he'd rather live there, so he moved back—this time to Krakow, Poland. To support himself, he set up an Internet-based translation company. Just what I needed.

I shot Thom an e-mail asking whether he had any contractors who could translate articles written in Arabic. Sure enough, he had a professor at the American University in Cairo. With the clock ticking, I sent the links off and crossed my fingers as my quest ventured off on yet another intercontinental leg.

She's My Grandmother

The gentleman who did the translations was thorough, so I soon learned more about Hoda's great-aunt. But what prompted a spontaneous happy dance on my part was his inclusion of a single comment posted by a reader. It said simply, "She's my grandmother."

A grandchild of Hoda's great-aunt? That would make this person Hoda's second cousin (though a genealogist's brain gets reasonably good at this kind of deduction, we're all beyond grateful for software that does the heavy lifting of sorting relationships for us). The translation included a version of the reader's name. I say "a version" because transliteration from Arabic to English can be complicated, but I at least had a good approximation of his name in English.

There was also no e-mail address from his posting, so now I had to figure out how to find him. If he posted here, he might have posted elsewhere, I reasoned, so I googled several versions of his name and clicked around the possibilities. His name wasn't especially common or rare, so there were plenty of hits to explore, but not so many as to discourage me.

Checking one version, I was slightly startled to find half a dozen men of that name on Facebook. Was it worth sending a message to a batch of strangers? The calendar was taunting me, so why not? I composed a note explaining who I was and what I was looking for and sent it off to all of them.

Much to my delight, one responded—Hoda's cousin. The search wasn't over yet because he was cautious. What ensued was something of a virtual interrogation. Who was I? Why exactly was I doing this? Did Hoda know? I didn't blame him. In

fact, I respected him for looking out for his cousin. Once convinced of my bona fides, he began to tell me about the family and
share some amazing photos.

Hoda's family, I learned, was an impressive one. Photos of her
parents' wedding showed President Nasser in attendance.
Another of her great-aunt included both Nasser and Sadat. But
it was a photo of her great-grandfather that intrigued me the
most. He was the one who had the foresight in the 1920s and
'30s to send one of his daughters to law school, and the other—
Hoda's grandmother—to med school. In fact, thanks to the assistance of Hoda's cousin, I was able to find the record of her
grandmother arriving in England to begin her medical studies at
the ripe old age of sixteen.

Did You Follow That?

Admittedly, this isn't conventional genealogy, but family history is constantly evolving, and social networking is one of the
newer tools we now have at our disposal. Had this all happened
even a decade ago, I probably would have been out of luck, but as
it was, I e-mailed a friend in Jerusalem, who called a cousin in
Cairo, who forwarded some googled links to me in New Jersey,
which I then shared with an American cousin in Poland, who
passed them on to a professor in Cairo, who shot the translations
to me back in New Jersey, where I Facebooked my way to Hoda's
cousin in Egypt, who digitized some wonderful family photos—
all in the space of one week, so that I could have something semi-
intelligent to say about Hoda's remarkable heritage on the *Today*
show. Phew!

CHAPTER SIX

A House Divided, a Bible Shared

The strange travels of a Civil War–era Bible

WE HAVE SO MUCH stuff in America that we often wind up with other people's stuff. It may be because you bought an old house and found a stash of letters tucked at the back of a shelf in one of the closets. It could be because you're an employee at a nursing home and the family mementos of a recently deceased resident were about to be tossed out since no relatives had stepped forward—and you couldn't bear to see that. Maybe you were surfing eBay or strolling through a flea market and found yourself captivated by a face gazing up at you from a photo taken a century or more ago. Perhaps you found some memorabilia slipped inside the pages of a used book at the local library's annual sale or got angry to find a Purple Heart at an estate sale and decided to do something about it.

I enjoy orchestrating the return of such family treasures to people who will care about them—more often than not, descendants of the original owners. I call this activity, an offshoot of conventional genealogy, orphan heirloom rescues, and I still remember my first time.

I was living in Vienna, Virginia, and stopped at a local antiques store where I spotted a nineteenth-century autograph album that once belonged to a teenage girl. It was $75—fairly steep for something I had absolutely no need for—but I couldn't bring myself to leave it there. Looking through the pages and reading the inscriptions written by her mother, sisters, and friends, I was reminded of my own mother's autograph book from her school days and was sickened at the thought of it sitting in a store waiting for a buyer. I had no choice; I purchased it and took it home with me. A month or so and a little sleuthing later, and I found myself having lunch with her great-granddaughter. She happened to live in the neighboring state, so I had the pleasure of presenting it to her face-to-face.

Rescuing Orphans

So started my peculiar sub-hobby. Initially, I sought out orphans to rescue. It was easy enough as they can be found in so many venues. Over time, I became more savvy, learning, for instance, not to give the item to a relative who lived close to where I found it. Doing so could mean that I was just giving an uncaring descendant a second chance to sell it.

At some point, I started writing articles about these orphan heirlooms and inviting readers to share the details about any articles in their possession that they wanted to return. Not long after that, I created a submission form on my personal website (honoringourancestors.com/apply_orphan.html), and in rolled the orphans. Photo albums, engraved silverware, war medals, letters, framed marriage certificates, inscribed books, diplomas, and Bibles—lots and lots of Bibles. It's not that genealogists are more religious than others. It's that we know how valuable the family record pages listing births, marriages, and deaths can be.

Time and time again, I did the detective work to track down likely recipients and then wrote about the search, as well as the happy reunion of the treasure with family members. Though I'm usually a virtual middleman in the process with the submitter sending the item directly to the family, I occasionally take possession and play deliveryman. Some of the more memorable cases for me involved giving a Bible once owned by a slave to one of his descendants and handing a 1930s photo album to the octogenarian it once belonged to—both perplexing and astonishing because it had been found on the streets of Jerusalem, though he was a New Yorker who lived in New Jersey and had never been to Israel. Nine years earlier, a woman had found it in the trash on the sidewalk, taken it inside, and kept it safe. When she passed away, her daughter contacted me. We never could solve the mystery of how it wound up in Israel, but it was a kick to watch the gentleman's face as he absorbed everything from a studio portrait of his long-deceased mother to hotel receipts from journeys taken decades earlier.

When I decided to write this book, it was a no-brainer that I would include one of the scores of orphan heirloom rescues I've tackled over the years. I've found that sharing this concept sometimes inspires others to do the same, and I like to think that amplifies the effect, and that on any given day, any one of us might get a call from a stranger offering a piece of our past for no other reason than it's a kind thing to do. Of course, I need to warn you should you decide to give it a go, it helps to have a thick skin because we can be quite, well . . . suspicious. To many, it's so unexpected that they instantly assume it's a scam. Especially when it comes to Bibles, prepare to be sporadically rebuffed by someone who doesn't listen long enough to understand that you're not trying to sell them religion. But if you can tolerate a dash of rejection from time to time, you're apt to find it very satisfying.

A Special Bible

With all the rescues I've done over the years, it was difficult to select just one, and oddly, the one I settled on stands out not so much because of the research required to track down the descendants of the orphan—in this case, a family Bible published in 1846. Though that's the aspect I usually emphasize, it's almost peripheral in this instance. Rather, I was taken with the story that spilled out of this special orphan.

The Bible was given to me by a fellow rescuer, Tracy St. Claire. Though hampered by health and other personal matters these days, Tracy once deliberately sought out Bibles with family records. You can still find almost 1,200 of them (and yes, she kept them all in her house) cross-referenced by name at bible records.com. If you take a look, you'll see that quite a few even include digital images.

Several years ago, to thank me for some now-forgotten favor, Tracy sent me a Bible from her collection. She had carefully chosen it because of an intriguing notation someone had written on an otherwise blank page near the front: "Picked up on Battle Field of the Civil War by Harvey Annis."

A Bible found on a Civil War battlefield? That seemed questionable, given that it weighed in at a hefty thirteen pounds, but how could any history buff resist? Some quick googling indicated that the Bible itself was quite rare, being the 1846 Harper's Illuminated Bible—said to be one of the most lavishly illustrated ever published. Though in poor condition, that meant it had some value, unlike most nineteenth-century Bibles, but truth be told, that didn't really matter to me.

Her Dear and Beloved Husband

Having inspected the battlefield comment, I turned to the dedication page. After "A Sacred Token from," Mary A. Williams had written her name. Further down the page beneath a delicate manger scene, she had identified the recipient as "Her Dear & Beloved Husband, Nathaniel Thomas Williams on the 28th of June A.D. 1847." Given the 1846 publication date, Mary must have been the original owner before bestowing it on her husband.

I turned to the following page and scrutinized a faded inscription near the top that someone else had duplicated immediately below in darker ink. It read (complete with capitalizations and a minor error):

> COPY OF ABOVE STATEMENT:
> This Sacred Book was given to me by my Dear and Beloved Wife on her death Bed with the request that I should read it attentively and try to meet her in Heaven. May the Lord so direct and instruct me to do so is the Prayer of her affectionate Husband. Oct. 1st 1847 (SIGNED) Nat. F. Williams

An involuntary gasp escaped my throat. Until then, I had been thinking of this Bible purely in Civil War terms, but now all I could think about was whether Mary had really dedicated the Bible to her husband the day she died. Turning to the page where deaths were recorded, I noted that the first entry was for Mary's father, who had passed away in May 1847. The second was for Mary herself: "Died at 8 minutes before 10 o'clock A.M. on Monday the 28th of June A.D. 1847 Mary Atherton wife of Nathaniel T. Williams."

I had my answer. The dates matched, and making comparisons, the handwriting definitely belonged to her husband. It didn't take long inspecting birth listings in the Bible to determine that Mary was thirty-three years old when she died. Seemingly in a hurry to rejoin her, Nathaniel passed away less than two years later and his death was listed immediately after hers. It's astonishing to find yourself choked up about a couple you had only learned of minutes earlier who departed this life more than a century before you were born, but that's exactly what happened to me. I took some comfort in knowing that Nathaniel's faith would have enabled him to almost happily contemplate his waning days as the precursor to the reunion he so hoped for.

Change of Hands

Perhaps because the couple was childless, they were essentially absent from the countless family trees avid genealogists have popped online. That made me reflect on these people who had been all but erased from memory. What would Mary think if she could somehow know that her tender inscription to her husband would provoke a stranger to write about them more than 160 years later?

This was interesting to consider, but their low profile also posed a bit of a problem. When they purchased the Bible, Mary and Nathaniel had recorded their own births. The next entry was for a Thomas Williams Mason who was born in 1839. With his middle name, I assumed that he was a nephew, son of a sister of Nathaniel's, but that was not the case. So how the heck was he connected?

I researched the possible relationships every which way I could imagine until I found an online citation from the Wilson Library at the University of North Carolina at Chapel Hill pertaining to a collection of Thomas Williams Mason's papers. It described Mason as "a lawyer and cotton planter who conducted the bulk of his professional activities in and around the town of Garysburg, Northampton County, North Carolina." The abbreviated bio went on to mention that he had served in the Confederate Army, was born at the Brunswick Plantation in Brunswick County, Virginia, and "was named for his first cousin, Nathaniel Thomas Williams, who may have been visiting Brunswick Plantation at the time. Williams gave his namesake the Huon Plantation located in Madison Parish, Louisiana, as a birthday gift."

This reference answered several questions. Now I knew that the Bible had once been owned by a Confederate soldier whose family had ties to North Carolina, Virginia, and Louisiana, and though I didn't realize it at the time, the comment about Louisiana would prove to be very useful down the road. Moreover, I now understood how the Bible had changed hands. Though first cousins, Williams and Mason were born in 1806 and 1839, respectively—a generation apart. By the time Williams visited Brunswick Plantation, he had been married for twelve years and remained childless. Possibly his Brunswick relatives were genuinely paying tribute to a favorite cousin or saw a future inheritance opportunity (I suspect a little of both), but whatever the reason, they named their newborn after Williams. Mason was only ten when Williams died, so regardless of which birthday he received the plantation for, it was an impressive gift by any standard. Along with the plantation, it seems, came the Bible.

Mason's Turn

The Bible's next owner, Thomas Williams Mason, accounted for a second run of entries in the Bible. His 1860 marriage to Bettie Gray was recorded, as were both of their births and that of their daughter, Sallie Williams Mason, who joined her parents on November 3, 1862. After that, the ink and the family name changed. In fact, there were no additional entries until 1871, which was curious because online family trees for this couple showed additional children born in the 1860s.

Before moving on, I decided to learn more about Mason, starting with his birthplace. Brunswick Plantation is now known as Mason-Tillett House and was added to the National Register of Historic Places in 2004, the result of the efforts of one of Mason's great-granddaughters who lived there until she passed away in 2010. In the application for the registry—which certainly made it easy for me to pick up the trail of his descendants—she noted that the house had been in the same family since the eighteenth century and that Mason was a judge who had served in both legislative chambers of North Carolina.

Nor was it difficult to determine that he had served in the Confederacy as a captain on the staff of General Robert Ransom, thanks to a brief summary of his life found in the necrology of his alma mater, readily findable with a bit of googling. That made my next find—his application for presidential pardon after the war—a bit of a surprise. In this 1865 letter to Andrew Johnson, he explained that he had "solicited Gen. Robert Ransom the privilege of becoming a volunteer aid on his staff." He had done so, he said, "for the purpose of avoiding the hardships of the service" that he believed would stem from an anticipated, "indiscriminate conscription."

The request had been granted and he had served until he took a leave of absence in November 1862 to visit his farm in Louisiana. He later attempted to rejoin General Ransom, but was refused. The letter went on to detail how he had managed to avoid service for the balance of the war by virtue of a pair of exemptions for which he qualified. He further acknowledged that he "has abandoned all claims to the service of his slaves in Louisiana and North Carolina," and that "those in Louisiana are farming for their own benefit on his lands there."

Of course, such a petition has to be taken with a grain of salt. To request a presidential pardon was a practical move, so Mason may well have taken liberties in his summarization of his wartime involvement or lack thereof. But the reference to Louisiana made me curious about the plantation he had inherited, so I made a quick check of the 1860 Louisiana slave schedules, which indicated that he had 206 slaves at the time. Little did I know that I would soon become better acquainted with some of these 206.

A Man of Letters

I tend to research in layers, delving deeper each time, so I made another round of searches before turning my attention to the next names in the Bible. By doing so, I found myself back at the website of the Wilson Library at the University of North Carolina, but this time, perusing a collection pertaining to Sally Long Jarman, a granddaughter of Mason's. Jarman was an enthusiastic genealogist, so her papers included random family documents, such as several letters Mason had written as a cavalryman in 1862. I e-mailed the library requesting a copy of these letters and was dazzled when they replied just hours later with digitized images (short, but important plea: please support our libraries and archives!).

I squinted my way through the correspondence, especially the one that amounted to hand-scripted plaid since Mason had written down the page, then turned it 90 degrees to write across—an attempt to cope with wartime paper shortages. It was in a letter to his father dated October 30, 1862 that he spelled out his intent to take a leave of absence to "make a trip to my plantation to see if I can't save something from the universal ruin impending even that part of our country." In the very next sentence, he conjectured that the war wouldn't last but another six months and said that he thought they could "very easily survive its savages" if they could just hold on.

Letters written the following month showed that he had indeed obtained that leave of absence and visited his Louisiana plantation, though I like to think that he was at least somewhat motivated by the birth of his daughter on November 3rd, the last Mason family event included in the Bible. It was plain that his primary objective was protecting as much as possible: "I intend to work and do the best I can, save all I can. If the enemy should come and destroy a part or all, that is what we can't help, but will have the satisfaction to know that I discharged my duty."

Louisiana felt safer to him than North Carolina, but not so

safe that he didn't trouble to move many of his slaves to Texas. In fact, one letter could be a peculiar kind of treasure to descendants of his slaves as he related to his father the specifics of why roughly two dozen of them remained in Louisiana. Jerry and Jack, it turned out, were "past the age for active labor," Big Cull had a stiff knee, and a cook with a name that appeared to be Pharaby was in delicate condition as she was "about the age for her monthly periods to quit her." As fascinated as I was, I reluctantly decided that the time had come to move on, but it would be interesting to revisit the letters to see if, say, Cull's descendants could be located. The fact that a letter in a North Carolina repository tells of slaves who lived in Louisiana who may or may not have gone to Texas says something of both the challenge and possibilities of African American genealogy.

Who's Harvey?

The next entry in the family records of the Bible was the 1871 birth of a Watson Lytle, apparently the son of James and Angelina Lytle. Given the 1862–1871 gap in birth listings, I suspected that this Lytle family might somehow be associated with Harvey Annis, the fellow who, according to the inscription at the beginning of the Bible, had picked it up on a Civil War battlefield. So I turned my attention now to him.

It took just moments to learn that he had served in the Union, though it would take longer to obtain his service and pension records to flesh out the details. Online Civil War soldier profiles indicated that he had enlisted in Company K, Wisconsin 18th Infantry Regiment in November 1861 and that he was commissioned as officer of Company G, U.S. Colored Troops, 51st Infantry Regiment in July 1864. These same online sources, however, failed to mention that he had been assigned to the Pioneer Corps (responsible for constructing roads and bridges and destroying enemy facilities, railroads and so forth) for roughly fifteen months in between. This made sense when I later learned that he was a carpenter by trade.

It was at this point that I realized that the Bible had been owned by both Confederate and Union soldiers. The battlefield claim in the Bible had hinted of this possibility, but now I was certain. It had changed hands and essentially changed sides, but I was curious exactly how the transfer had occurred. Before I would answer that question, though, the Bible had another twist in store for me.

The *Sultana*

Surprisingly few of us have heard of the sinking of the *Sultana*, America's greatest maritime disaster. Sure, we all know about the *Titanic* which resulted in 1,517 deaths, but the *Sultana*'s demise on April 27, 1865 caused the loss of roughly 1,700—and closer to 1,900 if you include those who initially survived but died shortly thereafter. More tragic still, the majority of those who were killed were former POWs, anxious to get home at the end of the war.

Timing and location conspired to keep the *Sultana* out of our collective memory. In historical terms, April 1865 was an eventful month. Robert E. Lee had surrendered and President Lincoln was assassinated. Our ancestors, who would have been slightly desensitized to large-scale death immediately on the heels of the Civil War, had other things on their minds when this disaster occurred on the Mississippi River slightly north of Memphis. Though the accident was extensively covered in local newspapers, it didn't attract the national attention one would expect given the scope of its impact.

Worse yet, it was largely due to greed. Tempted by the generous five-dollar-per-head fee offered by the government, captains bribed army officers to look the other way as they overloaded their steamboats in Vicksburg where Union POWs had gathered. The POWs, eager to get home, were willing to endure the packed conditions. In this manner, the *Sultana*, legally registered to carry 376 people, wound up burdened with closer to 2,500 passengers.

Before departure, a leak was noticed in one of the boilers, but rather than risk losing business to competitors by doing a proper repair, the *Sultana*'s captain, J. Cass Mason, ordered a patch job instead. The inadequate repair, coupled with the extreme weight of the load, caused three of the four boilers to explode at 2 a.m. on April 27th.

Among the victims were Lieutenant Harvey Annis and his daughter Belle. Among the survivors was his wife, Ann. I was incredulous to discover that the Bible that had already taken me on such an unexpected journey now led me to our country's worst maritime disaster.

Ann's Story

As the historic registration papers for the Mason-Tillett House had done for the Mason family, so a descendant's online account of the *Sultana* disaster provided a shortcut to finding living relatives—and not so incidentally, the Annis connection to it.

Great-granddaughter Helen E. Chandler had researched her family extensively and was fascinated with her English immigrant great-grandmother, Ann Vessey Laired Sims Annis. The reason for all the surnames? Ann was widowed three times, each time because her husband had drowned. According to Helen's account, Ann had survived two shipwrecks that had taken her husbands, the *Sultana* being one of them.

The Annis family features in just about any book or article you can find about the *Sultana*. You might, as I did, wonder why Ann was on the vessel with her husband in the first place. Harvey had become quite ill, so she had traveled from Wisconsin to

Vicksburg to nurse him. Leaving her older children at home, she brought their seven-year-old daughter, Belle. Ann and Belle remained in Mississippi with Harvey for eight months or so, partly due to his poor condition and partly due to bureaucracy. Though Harvey was trying to get discharged so he could return to Wisconsin, his papers had failed to arrive.

It was known that the orders had been signed and were en route, though, so the family decided to join the POWs and others on the *Sultana*. Since he still didn't have his discharge papers in his possession, Harvey continued to work even on the day of their departure and wore his uniform on board. Though they had a private cabin, the overcrowding of the steamboat didn't escape their attention, but they were reassured by an employee of the *Sultana* that it was safe, and as with the POWs, the urge to get home overrode their concerns.

On the evening of the 24th, the steamboat left Vicksburg. Two nights later on the 26th, it arrived at Memphis where it stopped to pick up coal. In the early hours of the following morning, the first two boiler explosions occurred, triggering fires, destruction, and chaos.

Tucked away in their cabin, the Annis family heard the tumult, and was swallowed in steam when Lieutenant Annis opened their door to investigate the situation. Slamming the door, he put life-preservers on himself and Ann, grabbed their daughter, exited the cabin, and steered his family to the stern. Ann's deposition records what happened next:

> He let himself down to the lower deck with the child, and I followed him, but as I was descending the rope a man from above jumped on me and knocked me in the hold of the vessel. From this I was extricated, and my husband, with our child, jumped overboard. I followed as soon as I could, but the life-preserver was not placed on me right and I held onto the rudder till I was obliged to let go by the fire.

About this time, Ann experienced the horror of watching her husband and daughter slip under the waters of the Mississippi River. They were never found.

Badly burned, she somehow managed to grab a piece of wood before losing consciousness and eventually waking up to find herself on the deck of a boat. She is believed to have been one of possibly only two female survivors.

Thrice water-widowed before the age of fifty, Ann returned to Oshkosh, Wisconsin, where she lived until 1900, but not without additional challenges. You might think that after all this that she would have been one of the first to be granted a widow's pension for the loss of her husband, but not so. Since her husband's discharge papers had been signed, though not received, the government rejected her claim, insisting that Harvey was not in active service at the time of his death. I waded through Ann's red-tape battles in Harvey's pension file in disbelief, stunned that this insult had been added to such conspicuous injury. The struggle finally ended in an Act of Congress specifically for the relief of Ann Annis, furnishing her with a monthly sum of $17.

Back to the Bible

Since the Bible still exists, it's evident that it was not with the Annis family on the *Sultana* that awful night, so I imagine that one day during her eight-month stay in Vicksburg, Ann shipped it to Wisconsin along with other items that might have been inconvenient to travel with. I can be quite confident of this because the balance of the family entries trace its ownership from Angelina Annis, oldest daughter of Harvey and Ann, to her son, Watson Lytle, and then to his daughter, Vera Leona May Lytle. Since she lived with her grandson Watson, it made me smile to realize that Ann had at least had the chance to enjoy the first three months of this great-granddaughter's life.

Vera lived until 1971, but never married, so it's sometime within the last four decades that the Bible slipped out of family hands. Providentially, it eventually found its way into the sheltering possession of Tracy St. Clair, who later passed it on to me. But one question remained: how had the Bible made its South-North transition—that is, how had it made its way from the Mason family to the Annis family?

This is where a close examination of military records and campaigns, supplemented by Google mapping, came into play. Not long after the Bible's last Southern owner, Thomas Williams Mason, had taken a leave of absence from the Confederacy to tend to his Louisiana plantation, Union forces had begun occupying plantations in this Louisiana river region, and were inundated by escaping slaves. The decision was made to lease some of the plantations and put the freedmen to work with the idea that proceeds from cotton and other crops could be used to pay for expenses. African American troops were designated to protect such plantations.

In his pension file, Annis is said to have been based at Goodrich's Landing in Louisiana. This fits since the 51st Regiment Infantry, U.S. Colored Troops, was attached to this post about the same time he was detailed to it and commissioned an officer. The 51st in turn, had been organized from the 1st Mississippi Infantry, which had been organized in May 1863 at Milliken's Bend, just slightly to the south. In short, it's likely that Annis now commanded some of the men who had been guarding the plantations.

Mason's plantation lay directly in the path between Goodrich's Landing and Milliken's Bend, on the one hand, and Vicksburg, where Annis would wind down his military career. In an affidavit by his widow, Ann, in his pension file, she described his work in stores and supplies, saying that he had "an order to draw rations from the contraband belonging to the Regiment that was left at Vicksburg." And in an 1871 claim the Bible's pre-

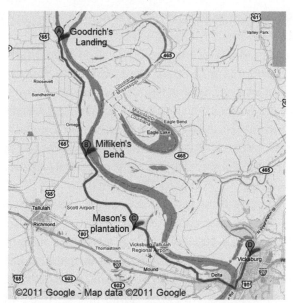

A map of the area sheds light on how, when, and where the Bible changed hands. (Google Maps)

vious owner, Mason, made to the U.S. Government, he sought reimbursement for stores taken from his plantation in May 1863. The petition, which was ultimately rejected, breaks down $31,300 worth of hogs, cattle, sheep, horses, mules, bacon, corn, fodder, and fuel he alleges was seized. It's not much of a stretch to imagine that a few personal items might also have been taken.

Scrutinizing the paper trails associated with both Mason and Annis, one can't help but notice the overlaps—stores and supplies, plantations, Milliken's Bend, etc. The most likely sequence of events, then, seems to be that the Bible was taken—possibly in May 1863—from Mason's plantation and found its way to Goodrich's Landing where Annis was stationed shortly thereafter. From there, he presumably took it to Vicksburg where it was shipped to Wisconsin avoiding a watery end.

Finding the Right Home

All that remains now is to find the right home. Normally, I return orphan heirlooms to their family of origin, but this one left
me with a dilemma: does it belong to the Mason family or the
Annis family? Given its dramatic history, it seems to me that both
families have a strong claim, and there are descendants in both
who have demonstrated ample interest in their family's past. The
good news is that there's no shortage of potential protectors for
the Bible.

But I couldn't bring myself to choose one family over the
other, so I have opted instead to find a suitable third-party home
for this orphan. Ideally, I'd like to see members of both the Mason
and Annis families come together as we commemorate the 150th
anniversary of the Civil War to jointly donate this extraordinary
relic to a repository such as the National Civil War Museum or
the National Archives, where it can be preserved and made available for the benefit of all. After all this Bible has endured, it seems
only appropriate that all of our grandchildren's grandchildren
should be able to hear its tale.

CHAPTER SEVEN

There's No One as Irish as Barack O'Bama

Tracing his roots to the Auld Sod

BEING A GENEALOGIST, I never expected my research to result in a presidential visit, the painting of an entire town, or one of those can't-get-it-out-of-my-head songs, but these were among the curious outcomes of this case. In fact, I've borrowed the title of the Corrigan Brothers song for the title of this chapter, but I suppose I should back up and start at the beginning.

Back in early 2007 as the presidential campaign was ramping up, I did some digging into the assorted candidates' ancestral pasts. That's when I discovered that Barack Obama, who was a relative newcomer on the national political scene at the time, was part Irish. In fact, on his mother's side, his Irish third great-grandfather, Fulmoth Kearney, is his most recent connection with any "old country" ancestry. When Fulmoth arrived in New York in 1850, all of Obama's other maternal ancestors were already here.

I shared my discovery and that St. Patrick's Day, Ancestry.com went out with a press release that noted, among other things, this fun fact. I was quoted, and since I have a unique name, it's easy to find me—and that's exactly what a number of Irish journalists did. Over and over, I was asked the same question: So he's part Irish, but *where* in Ireland did his ancestors come from?

The Irish Challenge

My mother's entire side of the family is Irish, and I was raised to be proud of my "auld sod" roots, so I wasn't unprepared for this interest. I knew that folks in Ireland would want to know exactly where. But Irish research is some of the most challenging there is. In terms of difficulty, I'd put it not far behind African American genealogy. This has to do with invaluable records that were destroyed in 1922, the fact that it was essentially illegal to be Catholic for long stretches of time (resulting in extremely patchy record-keeping), and the reality that government registration of births, deaths, and most marriages didn't kick in until 1864.

Other factors contributed as well, but the upshot is that to be successful at Irish research, you have to be able to identify the townland or parish that your family hailed from. That frequently creates a catch-22 situation because so many of our Irish ancestors came long enough ago (say, the Famine era in the 1840s and '50s) that the paper trail they generated post-emigration left no hint of their origins beyond the national level.

This created a bit of a conundrum for the Irish government, which, like many countries, is keen to promote tourism. While descendants of the global diaspora tend to have a soft spot for the land of their ancestors, they often won't visit Ireland until they know enough to be able to walk the same land their forebears once walked. It's no accident, then, that the Irish Ministry for Tourism, Culture, and Sport has recently embarked on a major digitizing initiative to make whatever records exist available for free online, but this much welcomed undertaking was too little, too late for my purposes. It didn't exist in 2007 and it wouldn't have gone back far enough to help with Barack Obama's roots even if it had.

Still, I was game to try to answer the question of which town would get the bragging rights. I just couldn't make any promises to the journalists who were doing the asking.

Finding Fulmoth

Obama's maternal roots run deep—in most branches for centuries—in America, so the initial stages of the research had been fairly straightforward. Using U.S. federal census records, conveniently generated every ten years starting in 1790, I marched back a generation at a time along his mother's side of the family. Decade by decade, I methodically plodded through every branch, all the while scanning for any hint of foreign-born ancestors.

One of Obama's great-great-grandmothers was named Mary Ann Kearney. She was interesting in her own right because I would eventually learn that she and her sisters Phoebe and Martha had married a trio of Dunham brothers—David, Jacob, and Jeptha—creating one of those families that makes me grateful for genealogical software to keep all the relationships straight. But for my immediate objective, what mattered most is that the 1870 census showed that her father, Fulmoth, was originally from Ireland. So he became my target and it was his place of origin in the old country I needed to somehow root out.

Though it's a bit difficult to read, he was recorded as Falmoth or Fulmoth, a name that would turn out to be a double-edged sword. Search-wise, it was a considerable hassle. Those with twenty-first-century expectations in terms of the accuracy of the spellings of our names might be surprised that I encountered countless variations of his first name—Fulmoth, Fulmouth, Falmouth, Fulmuth, Falmuth, etc. Compound this with a surname like Kearney, which randomly appeared as Carney or pretty much any way someone felt like spelling it on any given day, and I had to work the heck out of the wild-card functionality offered by the databases I was using (note to would-be genealogists: be prepared to show the "*" and "?" keys who's boss).

But at least his name stood out. As an Irish American with a Murphy branch in her family tree (Murphy being the most common surname in Ireland), I gladly accepted the nuisance factor of a name like Fulmoth Kearney in lieu of the "which one is he?" aggravation of sorting through an army of Daniel Murphys.

Fulmoth's Trail

With a little creative searching, I found him listed as Falmouth Carney (but indexed as Cainey) upon his arrival in New York on March 20, 1850 (curiously, I would later learn that one of Joe Biden's Irish ancestors, a shoemaker like Fulmoth, had arrived within five weeks of this date, causing me to contemplate the correlation between mid-century, Irish cobbler immigrants and politically inclined descendants). Highly unusual for that period, the ship's manifest included his destination of Ohio, an extra detail I hadn't expected.

Since he arrived early in the year, I crossed my fingers and looked for him in the 1850 census, which was conducted in August. Luck was with me and I found him in Wayne Township, Ohio, along with eight others named Carney, Cleary, and Canada all residing in the same household. While it seemed logical to assume that he might be kin to some or all of the others, the 1850 census did not include relationships, so I could only speculate.

It didn't take much more effort to pluck out additional records for Fulmoth. The 1860 census showed him married and living with his wife and four daughters in Deerfield, Ohio. The gap between the 1850 census (when he was single) and the birth of his first child (approximately 1853) gave me a narrow range of just three years to search for his marriage, which I found had

taken place in 1852. It was the 1870 census that led me to Fulmoth in the first place, and I discovered that he had passed away
in Indiana before the 1880, so now I had at least a bare bones
sense of his life in America. But nothing I had found so far gave
me any clue as to his hometown in Ireland, so I braced myself for
another layer of digging.

Surround and Conquer

Any good genealogist knows that if you can't find what you're
looking for regarding a particular person, it's time for a
surround-and-conquer approach—that is, attempting to back-
door into the information you're seeking by researching others
associated with your primary target. Clearly, it was time to try
this with Fulmoth and it didn't take much to get started. In fact, I
had already accidentally done it.

I mentioned earlier that it was rare for an 1850 arrival record
to include destination points for immigrants, but Fulmoth's did.
Those familiar with Irish American history could probably correctly predict that most of the Irish on the ship were heading to
New York—and they were, except two others who were also
going to Ohio. Imagine how pleased I was when I realized that
this couple, William and Margaret Cleary, were among the other
residents in the same house as Fulmoth later that same year in
Wayne Township, Ohio. This was too much of a coincidence to
easily explain away, so I was confident that there was a connection.

Focusing now on this pair of Clearys, I was startled to find
them in the 1860 census living with an older "Kearny" couple.
Well, older than Margaret, who was recorded as thirty-four years
old to William's sixty though the list of children that followed
strongly indicated that they were married. But why were they
living with Joseph and "Pharb" Kearney?

Until this point, I had regarded Fulmoth as the original

immigrant in this branch of Obama's family, but now it dawned on me that his parents might have also come to America. Looking at this census document, the most logical explanation was that Joseph and Phebe (which had been distorted into Pharb) were the parents of both Margaret and Fulmoth. That would explain why Margaret and Fulmoth had voyaged on the same ship, as well as why Margaret was living with Joseph and Phebe later on. Given that I also knew from following Fulmoth that he had named his oldest daughter Phebe, the pieces of the puzzle were beginning to come together.

Does Fulmoth Fit?

I was pleased at the prospect of Fulmoth's parents having come to America because it would mean still more people whose trails I could pursue in my search for a town in Ireland, but I needed to be sure that the family I seemed to be piecing together was truly a family. After years of genealogical detecting, I know how easy it is to be misled by the most reasonable-sounding assumptions, and I feel even more pressure than usual to verify every detail when I know my findings could be considered newsworthy.

I continued chasing records for each of the parties looking for evidence of relationships among them. Bit by bit, I assembled a family headed by Joseph and Phebe, including children named Margaret, Mary Ann, and William. Fulmoth seemed to fit in the mix, but I failed to find any records that confirmed him as being Margaret's brother, Joseph's son, or any other relationship that would have sealed the deal.

About this time, I managed to google my way to a well-hidden portion of a personal website run by a gentleman named Roger Kearney. Roger was an avid genealogist, and from all he had placed online, it was apparent that he was an excellent one. The good news for me was that he had information pertaining to

Joseph, Phebe, and the others, but the bad news was that there was no sign of Fulmoth. Had Roger been a sloppy researcher, I would have overlooked this, but the very fact that he was so skilled made me second-guess myself. If someone who had researched this Kearney family so thoroughly had no Fulmoth, then it was possible that I was simply wrong in trying to link him to this family.

What made this doubly frustrating was the fact that Roger's site included a tombstone transcription for Joseph Kearney that gave his birthplace in Ireland. If I could tie Fulmoth to these Kearneys, I would have what I was looking for!

Hoping against hope, I hired Carolyn Burns, an Ohio-based genealogist, to go to the cemetery where Joseph was buried to photograph every single tombstone. Maybe Roger had missed Fulmoth or chosen not to include him. Frankly, I doubted it, but it was worth a try. In the interim, I poked around Roger's pages for more clues and came across the 1848 will for a Francis Kearney. In it, he left land in Ohio to his brother Joseph, but only if he came to America to claim it. I found this interesting because the timing I was dealing with suggested a typical Famine-era emigration, but this will opened up a new possibility. If the Joseph mentioned in it was the same one I had been researching, then the instigation for the cross-Atlantic move was land.

Coming to America

The cemetery photos came back Fulmoth-less (though everyone else in the family was accounted for aside from Margaret), but I still wasn't willing to surrender my theory that he fit into this family, so I decided it was time for a trio of iffier tactics. I would try to piece together an immigrant saga for the Kearney family, see what Irish records might unveil, and track down living descendants to see if any of them held missing clues that could help.

If the 1848 will had prompted this family's departure from Ireland, I reasoned that there should be an immigrant trail to follow. I learned that the fellow who wrote the will died shortly after in 1848, so leaving time for word to get back to Ireland and arrangements to be made, I went looking for Joseph's arrival in America. Sure enough, there he was arriving in New York in April 1849—right name, age, and occupation.

One of the very first records I had located in this quest was the 1850 arrival of Fulmoth, along with Margaret and her husband, but what about Phebe and the other two children? More burrowing through databases turned up Phebe with Mary Ann and William landing in New York in August 1851. It was a classic case of chain migration. Dad comes first and makes a little money to send back for the oldest kids. Then they all work to earn the fare for Mom and the youngsters.

Fulmoth certainly seemed to be a part of the family, though I still couldn't rule out some quirky circumstance such as his being an adventure-seeking nephew who decided to tag along. I was well aware that others would have considered what I discovered so far to be sufficient, especially when taking the names of Fulmoth's children into account. Seven of the nine had names that could be tracked back to this family, but I needed more proof.

Murphy's Law

The tombstone for Joseph (as well as William's) gave the Irish birthplace as Moneygall. At the time, it would have been situated in Kings County, now known as Offaly. I didn't even know what religion the family practiced, but decided to have a go at church records. Although the odds were against it, I hoped to find the baptism of Fulmoth that would remove any doubt that he was the child of Joseph and Phebe.

Even when you know a place in Ireland, there's more work to be done due to a complicated system of overlapping townlands

It was tombstones in Ohio that told me where to look in Ireland.
(Carolyn Burns)

and parishes, so I enlisted the help of Kyle Betit, an expert in Irish genealogy. All told, there were more than a dozen parishes in the area, but Kyle methodically approached each one. No luck.

I suppose it was inevitable that the parish we needed would be the last on our list, but eventually, we were left with only the diocese of Limerick & Killaloe. We were fortunate that Stephen Neill, the Anglican priest who served there, was a bit of a techno-geek. His blog made him easy to find and communicate with, but Murphy's Law decided to have a little fun with us.

Were there records for the church in the necessary time frame? Yes, but the church itself had been closed some years ago, so the records were in the home of the church treasurer. Could he borrow them? Certainly. We waited—and waited.

To be a clergyman in Ireland is to be inundated with pleas from roots-seeking foreigners. Canon Neill was no different, and as he later remarked, "I get a lot of these requests and it was only

after the nature of the possible link with Senator Obama was revealed that I fully engaged with the search." We had kept the
Obama connection quiet as people can sometimes overreact
when celebrities of any kind are involved, but hoping to provoke
a swifter response, we finally shared it to the desired effect.

Thanks to the research I had done to this point, I had a wish
list of baptisms and marriages with names and estimated dates.
Now we just had to sit back and see if the records existed, but not
before being confronted with another complication. Sadly, the
treasurer who had the church books passed away while we were
back-and-forthing, so the matter of retrieving the records had
become more delicate. Eventually, though, Canon Neill had them
and looked up the names on my list in an index that someone
had fortuitously thought to create several decades earlier.

There was the marriage of Joseph and Phebe! There were the
baptisms of Fulmoth's siblings! Here finally was everything I had
hoped for—except Fulmoth's baptism. Murphy's Law had struck
yet again. Fulmoth's baptism did exist, but with one wee
problem—the wrong first name. The date and parents were
right, and there were no other couples in the parish named
Joseph and Phebe Kearney who needed to be ruled out, but the
record gave the child's name as Timothy.

If you're new to genealogy, you might think this means there
was a child named Timothy, but all indications are that it was
Fulmoth. The name was rare even in Ireland, so it would have
been easy to mishear or copy. Due to the flourish with which they
were often written, first letters in older script are notorious for
being confused with each other, and capital F's and T's are some
of the most commonly interchanged. Both names contained
"moth," and it's possible that Fulmoth simply didn't appeal to
the priest, so he tweaked it to the more conventional Timothy.
While it would be hard for us to accept today, clergymen in the
past often exercised some control over naming at christenings (in
my own family, I've encountered a priest in Eastern Europe who
gave illegitimate children unusual names to be sure that everyone

in the village knew and would never forget). There are many plausible explanations for the name being recorded as Timothy, but it certainly didn't help me.

Though I was more certain than ever that Fulmoth was a part of this family (and would later learn that Phebe's father was also named Fulmoth), I mourned the loss of the hoped-for baptism that would have made it so easy to prove to others. It's extremely helpful to have a single, smoking-gun document that makes it simple for everyone to grasp, but that wasn't to be.

Home Stretch

I considered the totality of what I had. Fulmoth appeared in records with his conjectured sister, Margaret, and she was definitely the daughter of Joseph and Phebe. The will-triggered immigration saga fit perfectly. He had named his children using typical Irish naming patterns that mapped this family's like a glove. His probable baptism record tied him to Joseph and Phebe, and he could have escaped ace genealogist Roger Kearney's notice simply because he moved on to Indiana, rather than remaining in Ohio with the rest of the family. Was this enough to declare victory?

The hunt for Irish records involved frequent wait-and-see periods, so I used those gaps to move forward with the last tactic of tracing descendants. It was through this somewhat tedious process that I would uncover the piece of proof that removed any remaining doubt for me, but which I've never shared until now.

Among the many branches of the family I followed was a genealogy buff who had uploaded a number of old photos. She wasn't a descendant herself, but had married into the family and come into possession of a stash of memorabilia. Much to my astonishment, that stash included a photo of Margaret, who had journeyed to America with Fulmoth in 1850, and on the flip side, one of her granddaughters had written her recollections of

Margaret. Margaret came across as a crusty, opinionated woman who wasn't terribly fond of her first husband, but what interested me more were fleeting references to *her brother*, "Fillie." I knew that Margaret had no brothers named Phillip, so this wasn't a case of mistaken identity. Fillie was Fulmoth, and he was indeed her brother. Yes!

Meeting the President

It certainly took some doing, but it was a pair of tombstones in a small town in Ohio that would ultimately solve the riddle of Obama's Irish roots and point the way to Moneygall. When I first drafted this chapter, I wrote of the pleasure I took in watching the ripple effect after my discovery was shared back in 2007. The media immediately descended on Moneygall and sporadically returned, mostly each St. Patrick's Day. As I had the opportunity to see for myself during a subsequent visit to Moneygall (thanks to Ollie Hayes for kindly opening his pub early!), the town proudly claimed its native son with signage and something of a shrine in Ollie's pub. Then-candidate Obama acknowledged his Irish roots in a letter he sent to be read at the dedication of Annie Moore's memorial (see Chapter 22, "Annie Moore, Ellis Island's First"), and continued to do so each St. Patrick's Day. There's been a book devoted entirely to his Irish roots, a film about his Irish heritage is in the works, and of course, there's the Corrigan Brothers song I mentioned at the outset.

It's a tradition for American Presidents to claim their Irish heritage and, likewise, for Ireland to claim them. JFK traveled to Ireland to a tremendous welcome, as did Reagan and Clinton. Even Nixon paid homage to his Emerald Isle roots. I had never envisaged that my research would trigger one of those classic, pint-in-a-pub moments, however, but that's exactly what happened. On St. Patrick's Day, 2011, during a White House visit by the Irish Prime Minister, Enda Kenny, President Obama announced his intention to travel to Ireland and visit his ancestral hometown of Moneygall. I was stunned and thrilled, and naturally decided I had to join the inevitable celebration myself. And so it was that my sister Stacy and I flew to Ireland.

We returned to Moneygall the day before the President's arrival and spent most of the day with Henry Healy, Obama's eighth cousin, by now known fondly throughout the country as Henry VIII. He and his family were gracious hosts through a bustling day that included perhaps a dozen interviews with CNN, ABC, *USA Today* and others. The world's media had engulfed this town of 297 inhabitants and they—and the rest of Ireland—couldn't have been more delighted.

The following day, while the Obamas raised a pint in Moneygall, Stacy and I joined the tens of thousands who stood for hours in on-and-off Dublin rain waiting their turn to see the president. We were well rewarded when he delivered an inspiring speech and tried out a few phrases of Gaelic—most notably, *"Is Féidir linn"* (Yes, we can). In their respective remarks, both Taoiseach Kenny and President Obama reminded the people of Ireland of all this small nation has endured, overcome, and contributed to the rest of the world—including America, where roughly 44 million claim Irish ancestry. *Is Féidir linn*, it turns out, travels well. In a country that's encountered considerable economic challenges of late, it was the right message at the right

President and Mrs. Obama thank the author at an event in Dublin.
(Stacy Neuberger)

time. It was, in short, a remarkably feel-good experience and I would have enjoyed being a part of it even if I hadn't been the instigator.

But the memory that will linger longest in my mind was when President and Mrs. Obama, along with the Kennys, personally thanked me. I was already flying high from the use of the g-word in a presidential address (seriously, how often do you think world leaders give genealogists a shoutout in their countless speeches?) when the foursome greeted me with hugs, kisses, and kind words. So yes, even though he's only 1/32 Irish, no one will ever convince me that there's anyone as Irish as Barack O'Bama.

CHAPTER EIGHT

Unclaimed Persons

Why you should call your estranged brother

ONE OF THE MOST USEFUL things I've ever done was almost accidental. It all started half a dozen years ago when I tripped across a newspaper article about the Lackawanna County coroner's office in Pennsylvania. The piece discussed several deceased people who seemingly had no relatives. Their identities were known, so these weren't John or Jane Does, but their next-of-kin could not be located. It was as if they had materialized from thin air, and that was creating problems for the medical examiner because he was legally mandated to make a best-faith effort to find and notify each individual's family. Until then I had been oblivious to what I quickly learned was a quiet epidemic: unclaimed persons. Think lost and found—only not for umbrellas and gloves, but for people.

Sadly, Lackawanna County isn't special in this regard. The problem is national in scope. If anything, major metropolitans and warmer locales have more to cope with because—a la *Leaving Las Vegas*—there really are places people go to die. That's not to say that all unclaimed persons fit this escape-from-life pattern. I suppose it would be possible to take an odd kind of comfort if that were so because we could convince ourselves that this phenomenon will never touch our own lives, but as I was to come to realize, there are many reasons that people go unclaimed and no family is immune.

What happens if no relatives can be found? Disposition of remains varies from county to county. Though most strive to respect traditions (for instance, those who served in the Armed Forces often receive a military burial and headstone courtesy of the Veterans Administration, and attempts are generally made to honor Jewish burial conventions for decedents known or believed to be of this faith), many are cremated. The cremains may then be buried (sometimes in registered containers so as to be retrievable in the future, sometimes not) in what amounts to a modern-day potter's field, scattered at sea or otherwise dispersed. Of course, increasing budgetary pressures are making it more and more difficult to provide even these basic services. Bottom line? Even in the best of circumstances, it's probably not what you would wish for yourself or loved ones.

My Initiation

The detail that caught my eye in the article I spotted was the mention of the family Bible of one of the deceased. Even with the names and birthdates of some relatives, the fellow's family had not been located. That's when I realized that I could help. In a sense, this was exactly what I had been doing for the army for several years at that point, but with a slightly more contemporary spin. Whereas the soldiers I research lost their lives in WWI, WWII, Korea, and Vietnam, these were present-day cases.

As has happened so many times in my genealogical career, I found myself making a peculiar cold call—this time to a coroner's office. I live in New Jersey, perhaps a two-hour drive from

Scranton, the county seat of Lackawanna, so I called and asked if I could come see the Bible. I explained that I might be able to find the man's family. Truth be told, I was expecting a polite brush-off, but they immediately invited me to the office. A few days later I went to retrieve one case and came home instead with a handful.

When I realized this wasn't a fluke situation, I googled my way around the topic and came across an online database of such cases for San Bernardino County, California. Dating back to the mid-1990s, it contained thousands of what it dubbed "un-claimed persons" (my introduction to the term) for counties across California, but mostly San Bernardino and Los Angeles. I selected several, used the same techniques I had honed working with the army to track down the decedents' families, and yet again, made a strange cold call. This time, I phoned the coroner's office in San Bernardino and supplied contact information for relatives to the slightly befuddled individual who answered.

Going Public

For several years, I continued to research Pennsylvania and California cases (in fact, I just received an e-mail with another from Lackawanna a few minutes ago)—a quiet, solo effort. Then in 2006, I launched Roots Television, a website of genealogical videos. My partner at the time suggested that my unclaimed per-sons sleuthing might interest viewers, so we produced a video about several of my cases. With the necessary travel and compet-ing demands, it wasn't until mid-2008 that we finally released the video, but once we did, we were deluged.

Genealogists are generous people, so as soon as they learned of this problem, they naturally wanted to help. While it may sound naïve, we hadn't anticipated this response, so we were left with a bit of a conundrum. On the one hand, our schedules were maxed out so we didn't have time to orchestrate a volunteer initiative. On the other, we didn't want to become a bottleneck to what could be a considerable resource to coroners and medical examiners across the country.

Several months prior to this, I had started using Facebook. Few genealogists were on Facebook back then, but I realized that I could create a group there that would otherwise take me a month or more to launch with its own website, so I popped one up and started steering those who expressed an interest to this group. So it was that many genealogists took their first halting Facebook steps in what was now formally called Unclaimed Persons. Several months down the road, I developed a companion website, but the heart of the group continued to function on Facebook.

Though the last thing I had time to do was to administer such a group, that's exactly what I wound up doing. The learning curve was steep as there were soon hundreds of zealous volunteers whose research needed to be guided. Procedures had to be established to verify findings, assure that no families were directly contacted (that was the domain of the coroners), and avoid redundant effort. In their hunger to assist, some had taken to cherry-picking cases off San Bernardino's database, the problem being that the same ones were being solved repeatedly—a situation that unintentionally created *more* work for the county for a while.

Courting the Coroner

In the early days, I found myself in the peculiar position of having to round up more cases to satisfy the eager volunteers, which was more difficult than you might imagine because we were a new and unproven entity. In spite of offering our services for free, I had to conduct something of a courtship with each coroner's office, sometimes requiring months to convince them to give us a few trial cases.

I liken it to publicly admitting that you like Barry Manilow. No offense, Barry—I'm a lifelong fan—but let's be frank: it takes courage to admit that you're a Fanilow because to do so is to invite scorn from a certain contingent. Similarly, some coroners were reluctant to admit that just maybe a bunch of amateur genealogists could do something they couldn't. I suspect some feared a perception that they weren't trying hard enough in their efforts to locate next-of-kin, but the reality is that the methods and resources used by genealogists are largely complementary to those used by law enforcement and other public officials. They can find relatives Unclaimed Persons probably can't, but the reverse is also true. We were one more tool being put at their disposal, but it took time for some to warm to us.

Passing the Baton

Gradually, a system emerged, case administrators were appointed, and a website—complete with case counter—was set up. Word of the group was starting to spread so coroners, rather than waiting to be approached, were sometimes reaching out to us. Although I hadn't intended to create or manage such a group, I did so for the first year until it got on its legs. But it truly was turning into another full-time job, so I carefully observed the contributions of the members and selected three I thought would be ideal to take the reins. Luckily for me, Janis Martin, Skip Murray, and Keri Maurus all agreed when requested, and today, the group continues to be guided by the tireless duo of Janis and Skip.

As of this writing, 240 cases have been solved, although I'd like to think the number will have jumped considerably by reading this. You can check if you'd like at www.UnclaimedPersons.org. For my part, I continue to spread the word and do what I do best—solve cases.

If you'd like to give your gumshoe skills a workout and

contribute your services, click the join option at unclaimed persons.org and follow the instructions. You'll be asked to agree to a set of guidelines, and once you do, you're welcomed to the team. After that, it's your choice whether to sit back and observe for a while or to jump in on some of the currently posted cases.

Not Just Other People

Even if you don't join, please consider telling others—if not about this group, then at least about this issue. Awareness will go a long way to addressing this problem because contrary to what many may think, this isn't something that happens to other people.

It's easy to tell ourselves that becoming an unclaimed person is the outcome of succumbing to addictions and the criminal activities often used to support them. You'd be right in many cases, but the philosophy of Unclaimed Persons is that every life is worth remembering. Even those who have hurt their loved ones through their choices in life are usually remembered and missed by someone.

One case I worked on involved a man who got into drugs and consequently became an absent father. He was identified when his teenage daughter, who hadn't seen him since she was a little girl, traveled with her mother from Florida to the morgue in Pennsylvania. Though years had passed, they knew it was him because he had their names tattooed on his arm. Knowing that he loved the ocean, they took his remains and arranged a ceremony at the beach—a tribute to the man they remembered before he took a wrong turn.

It's often said that funerals are really to comfort the living, and the same could be said of this work. Time and time again, coroners report that relatives who haven't seen the deceased for years are very grateful to be informed. "Now they don't have to wonder anymore" is an oft-repeated phrase.

So what else aside from bad choices can cause someone to wind up unclaimed? You'd be surprised. Here's a sampling:

- Some end up unclaimed because they have wanderlust—say, make a living as a trucker—and family members become accustomed to only hearing from them once in a while. By the time someone notices that it's been years since the last contact, the wanderer may already be long buried in some distant place.

- Venturing alone from another country increases your odds of eventually joining the unclaimed, especially if you don't keep in touch with those back home.

- As you might expect, living alone and outliving everyone in your generation can place you in the company of the unclaimed.

- Frequent moves and multiple marriages (for women) can be contributing factors simply because those who care eventually lose track of addresses or can't keep up with the latest surname. I recall a British woman who had six marriages and six children, but was still among the unclaimed when she died in Florida.

- Call it poetic justice, if you like, but those who steal others' identities tend to find themselves unclaimed as their deaths often expose their subterfuge, but not their original name.

- Name changes for reasons other than marriage or identity theft can also factor in. One man I researched turned out to have been at the center of a notorious paternity suit that played out in the newspapers for about five years in the 1930s. In an attempt to bolster her case, his mother named him after the prominent man she had an affair with. Later in life, he changed his first name, most likely to separate himself from the controversy. Unclaimed by his father at birth, he ironically wound up unclaimed at death because his name change had masked his identity.

• It's a sign of the times, I suppose, that there are those who hop a bus to go elsewhere to die when terminally ill because they don't want their families to have to bear the burden of their health-care costs.

• Frankly, our lives have just become so darn busy that we're not as good at keeping in touch—even with those who mean a lot to us—as we used to be. And that simple reality, the loss of community, plays a role.

• Feuds triggered by minor incidents are also a common theme. I first encountered this in an early San Bernardino case involving a decedent found in a Jeep in the desert in, as the coroner described it, "less than favorable condition." Research quickly revealed that he was the youngest of seven children in a close Mormon family, but only one brother remained. Because we featured it in the video, we received permission in this one instance to speak with this brother who hadn't heard from "little Joe" for half a century. Why? Fifty years ago, Joe had stayed at his house, and while shaving one morning, refused to get out of the bathroom to let his four-year-old nephew use it. That sparked a spat that morphed into a full-blown feud. The nephew is now in his midfifties, but that trivial incident had separated the family for decades.

What You Can Do

The silver lining in all this is that this quiet epidemic could be drastically curtailed through increased awareness. And the solutions are easy. If you're so inclined, Unclaimed Persons would welcome your support as a volunteer, of course, but how about making it a habit to check in with that annoying brother of yours each holiday season? You don't have to mend fences; just keep track of each other. If you live alone, use a magnet to put the names and phone numbers of a few relatives on your refrigerator, display several family photos (with names on the back) around your home, or exchange some family details with friends and neighbors (coroners often consult them to find relatives). If you have any elderly relatives living alone or in a nursing home, send a postcard on vacation or a holiday card each year (your return address might just be how the coroner finds your family). And the next time you get a card or letter returned in the mail from a loved one, take the time to investigate. Simple steps like these can help ensure that no one you care for will ever join the ranks of the unclaimed.

CHAPTER NINE

Adventures in TV Land
You need what *by* when*?!*

MY VERY FIRST GIG in the genealogical world was as lead researcher for a PBS television series called *Ancestors*, and I have a long-deceased, Zanzibari princess to thank. Since then, I've researched for (and usually appeared on) *Who Do You Think You Are?*, *Faces of America*, *Top Chef*, *African American Lives*, *Ancestors*, *Timewatch*, *They Came to America*, as well as many popular talk and news shows such as the *Today* show, *Good Morning America*, *The Early Show*, *Fox News*, CNN, and *BBC Breakfast*. But it was Princess Salme who started it all. Perhaps I should explain.

Though I've been a genealogist since the sixth grade, it seemed like a fantasy to try to make a living at it when I wrapped up my education, so I went into the consulting industry. As an international marketing specialist, I traveled extensively, often to developing countries. The 1990s found me bouncing around a number of places including India, Ukraine, and Tanzania. At one point, I averaged nine months a year overseas, but somehow during the stints back home, I managed to find time not just for genealogy, but also for another hobby—television production. Nothing fancy, mind you. Local access TV.

After a few years of this, I decided it was time to graduate from the local access world, and set my sights on producing a documentary. Typical of me, I couldn't just interview the interesting woman down the street. Nope. I had to set my sights on a Zanzibari princess who eloped with a Westerner back in the 1800s (how Disney has missed this real-life, multicultural princess, I'll never know).

I had first encountered her during a business trip to Dar es Salaam when I impulsively took a ferry to Zanzibar for the weekend. There I quickly learned that the two most famous Zanzibaris were Freddie Mercury and Salme, and I was captivated by her story. So began my documentary project, which went amazingly well—so well, in fact, that I quickly got in over my head. Needing advice, I contacted the only "real" (that is, not local access) producer I knew at the time, a woman I had met in the West Bank of Palestine when she was making a film on the Dead Sea scrolls and I was on a consulting assignment. I was living near Washington, D.C., when I called her, and as luck would have it, her partners were there for a PBS conference, so she suggested that I get together with them.

I met with this pair of producers the next day for the purpose of picking their brains about my documentary, but during the course of dinner, it came out that they were about to begin producing another season of *Ancestors*, a series that's much beloved by genealogists who have been at it for more than a decade. At the mention of the show, I did what any good genealogist would do if you give them a chance—babble incessantly about every aspect of family history research. And that, I thought, was that.

My First Show

A few months later, I woke up to an e-mail saying, "We know this sounds crazy, but could you come to Provo tomorrow?" The production was being done by KBYU, based in Provo, Utah, and their lead researcher had abruptly left the project, putting them in a world of hurt. This was back in the dark ages of 1999 when TV seasons were mostly thirteen episodes long. They needed thirteen stories for the next season and they needed them fast. Not sure what to do, they flashed back to that evening when I prattled on at dinner. Recognizing my enthusiasm for the topic and knowing that I had at least a basic knowledge of television production, they rolled the dice and offered me the slot. I was on the plane the next day, making me probably the only person in the world who can say that she went to Provo by way of Palestine and Zanzibar.

This was my introduction to the intense life of feeding the television content machine. Working on this first show back in the days when many still weren't online, I got my hands on every story I could, any way I could. Sure, I put solicitations out on the Internet, but this was long enough ago that the 5,000 or so responses I got annoyed my e-mail provider at the time. I also requested and received just about every past issue of every genealogical magazine ever published. My hotel room was crowded with stacks of back issues, undoubtedly a fire hazard. I did whatever I could, worked the phone nonstop, and called in every favor ever owed to me.

In the end, I found so many stories that we now had a new problem: there were simply too many good ones to squeeze into the show. That's when I got the notion to do a companion book to share more of them. Given the green light, I snagged some books on writing book proposals, whipped one up, researched a bunch of agents, and found the perfect one (thanks, Linda!) who landed me my first book deal a whopping two weeks later. It didn't hurt that another unrelated event landed me on the *Today* show, my first television appearance, around this same time. Serendipity, intertwined with lots of hard work, runs through my genealogical career—and that's a good combination if you're on a mission to get the G-word out there.

What to Expect

I'm frequently asked by fellow genealogists what it's like to work on TV shows, so I thought I would lift the cover and provide a peek. Due to non-disclosure agreements that could haunt me for the rest of my life, I can't discuss many specifies, but sharing my experience at a broader level will give you a flavor.

Out of the Blue

Almost every show I've worked on has come up abruptly. For some reason, that translates to Friday afternoon phone calls for me. Whether the producer is in London, New York, or California, the initial contact tends to occur just as we're heading into the weekend, and I rather enjoy that as it gives me something fun to mull over. Sometimes it's just a feeler call to sound me out, but as often as not, they need me to start working immediately. For that reason, if you aspire to do this kind of work, get used to working without a net as you'll frequently have to jump into the research right away and trust that the contract will materialize. The good news is that while I often wind up fronting the research time and costs, I've never *not* been compensated.

Intensity

The pace on just about every show I've worked on is fairly manic. Those episodes of globe-trotting celebrities—and even those three-minute segments you see on morning shows—are the proverbial tip of the iceberg. Typically, hundreds of hours of research have gone into each one because the standard approach is to research the entire family tree (or history mystery, as the case might be) and then select only the most interesting bits for TV. What makes it to air might reflect perhaps 5 percent of the research that was done.

Because the research phase of these shows tends to be such a whirlwind, I didn't really have a good sense myself until I decided to track my time on the last show I tackled. What I discovered is that I averaged 19.5 hours a day, seven days a week. Some don't fully grasp how mainstream genealogy has become, so they still retain outdated notions of what it is to be a genealogist. Consequently, even those featured in the shows don't always appreciate the reality of what's gone into their segment or episode. I recall one occasion when I had just finished taping a cameo for a show (you know, those talking-head experts?), and the person who interviewed me remarked, "Now you can go back to your sleepy life." As if! She was only right in the sense that once the research is done, I make an effort to catch up on all the sleep I've missed.

Happily, I love what I do so much that I don't notice the hours flying by, and I don't mind putting other plans on hold until we reach the finish line. Somewhat perversely, I thrive on the insane deadlines involved (and I'm lucky enough to have a husband who tolerates an AWOL wife), but this isn't for those interested in making a little extra income surfing the Internet after-hours.

Role of the Genealogist

With a dozen or so shows behind me, I can tell you that the genealogist generally plays one of two roles. Either you're a valued member of the production team (BBC and *Top Chef* are my all-time favorites for just this reason) or you're put into what I refer to as go-fetch mode, meaning that you will mostly be seeking items on producers' wish lists.

Some genealogists do very well in a go-fetch environment. In a sense, it's less stressful because the pressure is mostly on the producers and your responsibility is simply to do the best you can retrieving desired documents. But I do best when I'm given the freedom to completely immerse myself in a family tree and dig up whatever I can. My research has made front-page news on several occasions, and in each instance, I had free rein.

I believe that there's no such thing as a boring family, so I see my job as plunging in as deeply as I possibly can, exploring every branch, and letting the stories reveal themselves. But this organic approach can be stressful for producers who are on the hook for a completed story, so they often prefer to have as much control as possible in order to reach that goal on time. So I completely understand the wish-list mentality, but revel in those opportunities I have to work with producers who are brave enough to trust the outcome!

How It's Done

The not-so-exciting corollary to the frantic pace of the research is that in addition to being an excellent genealogist, you had better excel in project management and networking. Particularly for large-scale undertakings such as an entire series, there's no way one genealogist can do it all. Even for smaller initiatives, chances are that the necessary clues are scattered in a variety of locations, and time and budget constraints usually mean it's impractical for a single genealogist to take it all on. In spite of what many think, what's online is still only a tiny fraction of what's available so if you don't get feet on the ground in multiple places, you're almost definitely leaving compelling stories untold.

In my former life as a management consultant, I orchestrated projects on an international level. By way of example, I once ran a World Bank project to improve the quality of steel production in India, and that experience is oddly germane—in fact, invaluable—to working on TV shows. Confronted with one month to research the sailors who lost their lives in the USS *Monitor* during the Civil War (as described in Chapter 13), I coordinated the efforts of nineteen researchers across the United States, Canada, England, Scotland, Ireland, Denmark, and Australia. And that's the approach I use on all of the shows I work on.

I think of myself as the center of a bicycle wheel with each of the spokes being another researcher. I do the preliminary research and develop a list of requests that I shoot out to assorted researchers. As each request is fulfilled, I digest and assimilate the incoming information and formulate a fresh batch of targets. One document arriving from the Family History Library in Salt Lake City, for instance, might result in three more solicitations going out to researchers in Boston, Washington, D.C., and Dublin. Now multiply this by countless overlapping assignments. In project management jargon, there's a lot of sequencing and simultaneous engineering going on. You have to know genealogy cold so you can quickly assess what genealogist A needs to snag (say, a death date from a tombstone in a cemetery) before you can ask genealogist B to look for something else (say, a corresponding obituary or will) so you can complete all the research as efficiently as possible. At any given time, you're juggling dozens of such mini-tasks (often for each of several celebrities) in order to keep that research wheel moving forward at all times.

That's why it's also helpful to have a well-developed network of researchers. Luckily for me, a decade of traversing the country on the speaking circuit—mostly lecturing at libraries and genealogical societies—means I have just that. That, supplemented with social networking and my former globe-trotting career, helps me consistently deliver what even I might first think is impossible.

Perks and Frustrations

I suppose it's obvious that it's pretty darn cool to see your handiwork on air, and even more so when someone well-known visibly and emotionally reacts to what they learn about their heritage. One of the stranger aspects of genealogy is that I often wind up learning information about people's families that they don't know themselves, so it's almost like being a retro-psychic, and it's gratifying to see how folks respond. That's doubly true when I have the chance to be there in person.

Several years ago, when I did a series of roots segments with the then-hosts of *Good Morning America*, I taped segments with Diane Sawyer, Robin Roberts, Sam Champion, and Chris Cuomo, but it was Robin who invited me to be live on air. This was unexpected because she had been the least interested at the outset. Due to her African American ancestry, she suspected that little could be learned, but when the research traced her Roberts line back to the 1700s, she became a convert. Ultimately, Robin was the only one of the four to squeeze in a trip to walk in her ancestors' footsteps, and though it was edited out, at one point in our interview, she and I had our arms slung around each others' shoulders and were singing "Kumbaya"! She totally got it—the pull of genealogy and what makes it so fascinating to so many—and to have a part in that transformation was more than I could have hoped for.

But frequently, the genealogist has to accept that their contributions will be anonymous. For instance, there's a celebrity who will never know that it took me less than twenty-four hours to find their long-missing grandparent, and that's just the way it is. Not surprisingly, some discoveries won't make it to air. In fact, some won't even make it as far as the celebrity, as happened when I found a bunch of previously unknown cousins for one. Sharing that would have meant admitting that Grandpa had a secret, second family, and that wasn't the direction this show wanted to go. In that case, I didn't mind that this didn't become part of the story, but I do regret that this individual still doesn't know about these relatives. But again, that's the way it is.

As with everything, there are upsides and downsides, but to me, it's all worth it if it helps genealogy garner a little attention and attract fresh recruits. Back in the 1970s, the miniseries *Roots* first introduced genealogy to a broader audience, and even with all the alternatives we have today, television continues to be the best way to get others excited about heritage-hunting. To me, the more family history playmates we all have, the better, so if the phone rings next Friday afternoon, you can be sure I'll answer!

CHAPTER TEN

Finding Melvina, Michelle Obama's Great-Great-Great-Grandmother

How do you trace a slave girl in South Carolina?

IT'S RARE THAT I devote eight months and thousands of dollars of my own money to research someone else's roots, but Michelle Obama is one of those cases. Some of my discoveries about her ancestry eventually made their way to the front page of the *New York Times*, the second time my research would stake a piece of that territory (Annie Moore, the first to arrive at Ellis Island, being the first). Though I did more interviews than I can recall after the fact, what's curious to me is that no one asked how I did it. While I appreciate that level of confidence in my work, I'd like to share some of the behind-the-scenes detective work because—well, Michelle Obama's ancestors made me work for it!

And I like that. I appreciate it when our forebears make me apply some elbow grease to smoke out their secrets. If I can click my way to the answers I seek, I get bored, but Mrs. Obama's family tree was one of the most challenging I've ever climbed and I enjoyed every minute of it.

Why I Did It

Why did I decide to trace the then about-to-become First Lady's roots? Jodi Kantor, a reporter for the *New York Times*, triggered my interest. Shortly before the January 2009 inauguration, she contacted Henry Louis "Skip" Gates Jr., Harvard professor and well-known host of several PBS genealogy series. I worked with Skip on *African American Lives* and *Faces of America*, so he was familiar with my tenacious research style and directed her to me. Could I, Jodi wondered, look into Michelle Obama's heritage for an article she was writing?

I could and did, but time was short, so I could only find out so much. I shared what I managed to unearth so swiftly, and Jodi kindly gave me a shout-out in the resulting piece. But unbeknownst to her or anyone else, I kept going after the article was published.

There were several reasons for this, the primary one being that I regard the presence of Michelle, Malia, Sasha, and first grandmother Marian Robinson, in the White House as historic. They are the first descendants of slaves to reside in the White House as members of the first family, and in my opinion, that's a big deal. In a period of less than 150 years, to progress from slavery to 1600 Pennsylvania Avenue speaks volumes about this family and our nation. Distracted by the rush of our everyday lives, we might shrug it off today, but a hundred years from now, historians will be discussing this precedent.

On a personal level, one of the first details that caught my attention was the fact that Marian Robinson's maiden name was Shields. My own mother's name was Shields, so I have a bit of an affinity for others with this name. Mind you, I didn't expect that there would be any relationship between our families because my Shields arrived in the 1880s from Northern Ireland. But just as I found myself drawn to Brooke Shields while researching episodes of the NBC series *Who Do You Think You Are?*, my interest ratcheted up a few levels when I spotted this surname in the mix.

I also admired the freshly minted First Lady, which to be honest, was a factor as I wouldn't independently invest significant effort into someone's roots otherwise.

The final reason I felt compelled to research Michelle Obama's ancestry is because it hadn't been done. Perhaps I should qualify that statement a bit. There were actually quite a few articles and TV segments that had been done on her roots when I started, but every last one of them concentrated on her Robinson branch from Georgetown, South Carolina. I got that. Robinson was the name she was born with so I could understand starting there, but what I couldn't grasp is why everyone stopped there.

To give you some idea of why this perplexed me, by the time I was done tracing all the branches of her family tree back four or five generations, this portion that had been investigated earlier would account for less than 15 percent of her heritage. And though she had roots in at least eighteen communities scattered across eleven states (she's the Great Migration wrapped up in one person), all the prior focus had been solely on Georgetown.

This astonished me until I did a little digging. Many genealogists enjoy researching celebrities' family histories, and presidential families are among the most heavily explored, but everywhere I looked, I found false starts. Plenty of would-be trees included Michelle Obama, but sported just a stubby branch or two. In fact, except for her Robinson branch, most failed to get past her parents. Why? Because her family was extraordinarily hard to find.

Her family offered up every sort of roadblock you could imagine, so I was hooked immediately. This was the genealogical version of being the first to leave a trace in the deep snow that's blanketed the town, and I couldn't resist the chance to break the trail in unplowed territory!

The Shields Branch

When I contacted the *New York Times* to tell them that I had excavated considerably more of the First Lady's genealogy, I suggested that they focus on the Shields branch. Given what I've just shared, this won't surprise you, but it wasn't simply because of my attachment to the name. Whenever you research anyone's history, there are always certain ancestors who seem to clamor for your attention, to call out louder than others—and that was the case with her Shields line.

It had taken some doing to wade back through the generations—Michelle to her mother, Marian; Marian to her father, Purnell; Purnell to his father, Robert; and Robert to his father, Dolphus. That made Dolphus Theodore Shields (who preferred to go by "D. T.") Michelle Obama's great-great-grandfather, and I found him intriguing. Like many of her other ancestors, he was hard to follow, partly because he had married at least four times. It's not that he was a womanizer; in fact, all the evidence suggested that he was a strict, disciplined sort of fellow, having bought his own home, owned his own business, and helped establish several Baptist churches. But he enjoyed a long life, and outlived a couple of wives along the way.

D. T. lived until 1950, so I wrote to the Birmingham Public Library for his obituary, and was impressed to find it on the front page of the newspaper. This told me how well respected he must have been in the community. The article noted that he had recently celebrated his ninety-first birthday, having been born around 1859, and the day he died, the headline read, "U.S. Court Bans Segregation in Diners and Higher Education."

I let that sink in. Born into slavery, Dolphus had lived long enough to witness the first steps of desegregation. Even more remarkably, I realized that this meant his life had overlapped with that of his great-granddaughter, Marian Shields, who would go on to live in the White House. I don't know if he ever met his Chicago-born descendant, but I'd like to think that she spent a

summer in her youth visiting her Alabama relatives and that the
two came face-to-face.

Meeting Melvina

Because his name was so distinctive, it was easy to step back
another generati▓▓▓▓▓▓▓▓ D. T. to his mother, Melvina. I found
them together in the 1870 census, the first to enumerate former
slaves under their full names.

Sometimes a single document can speak volumes and this is
one of them. "Melvinia Shields" was living in Clayton County,
Georgia, along with Dolphus and three other children, Jane,
Allice (sic), and Talley. Though ages should always be taken with
a grain of salt, the census indicated that she was born around
1844 in South Carolina.

Living side by side with Melvina's family were Charles M.
Shields and his wife and daughter. They were recorded as white,
while Melvina was listed as black, but I couldn't help but notice
that Charles was the only other person who had been born in
South Carolina. He and Melvina were surrounded by native-
born Georgians. More curious still, Melvina's children were
listed as being mulatto—all except Talley, who was listed as

*If carefully inspected, this 1870 census record reveals many details about
the First Lady's family.* (National Archives and Records Administration)

black. This made me laugh because another notation specified that he was a twin to "Allice." I gathered that the census taker was going by personal observation.

Reading between the lines, this hinted that Charles might have been the father of some or all of Melvina's children—particularly because my later research would show that this was the only time that Melvina appeared under the name Shields, though her children consistently used the name. In all the other documents that include a surname for Melvina, her surname was given as McGruder. Through DNA testing, it would be possible to determine whether Charles, or at least, a white Shields ██████████████ather of Melvina's child. If he was the father, then Michelle Obama, like her husband, is part-Irish. Having played with DNA for years, I could have pursued this line of investigation, but I was more curious about Melvina herself. Where did she come from and what was her story?

Finding Melvina

Additional records I found about Melvina's later years reinforced the notion that she had been born in South Carolina in the early 1840s, but let me ask you this: How do you go about finding a slave girl named Melvina in South Carolina?

Believe it or not, no one ever asked this question. Perhaps those who have never done any genealogy think there's some magical, master index that lists every slave who ever lived, but as anyone who's ever done any African American family history research can tell you, it can take years to find an ancestor pre-Emancipation, and there's no guarantee that you'll ever succeed. So how exactly did I find Melvina?

I started by making the assumption that whether Charles was the father of Melvina's children or not, there was seemingly some connection between her family and his. And since both she and he had been born in South Carolina, I thought that she might have once been owned by his family. Bearing this in mind, I researched his family and determined that they had migrated to Georgia from Spartanburg, South Carolina. This narrowed my search range from the entire state to one county, but there was still much more to do.

Sadly, when looking for enslaved ancestors, it's necessary to troll through property records where they'll frequently be listed in wills, deeds, and inventories along with other possessions such as wagons, tools, furniture, animals, and crops. Thinking that Melvina was most likely owned by the Shields family, I searched all the likely records for those named Shields in Spartanburg, but came up empty.

This was a disheartening moment. At this point, I had been researching Michelle Obama's family for months—coming up against brick wall after brick wall, and brainstorming ways to clamber over them. As I mentioned earlier, I generally thrive on this kind of uphill battle, but frankly, I was tired. Aiming to find a handful of generations across her entire family, I was finally on the home stretch and didn't know if I had the stamina to navigate this obstacle. Not finding Melvina mentioned in Shields papers meant that I had to cast the net wider and start searching for any signs of a girl named Melvina in the whole county.

I gritted my teeth and got back to work. After spending some time flailing around on this needle-in-a-haystack quest, I decided to go back to basics to see what resources might be available to help me. True, many of the property records for Spartanburg were indexed, but that didn't make things any easier since I didn't know what the owner's name was. But then I took a second look at the South Carolina State Archives website and realized that they had done something that might just make a difference. The coverage was patchy, but they had indexed some property records across the state. The revelation was that they had also indexed the names of slaves mentioned in most of the records! Brilliant!

Melvina wasn't a common name at the time, but it wasn't

rare, and the system wasn't quite as user-friendly as I would have liked, so I had to search for Melvina, Melvinia, Malvina, Malvena, and every variation I could think of. By working the database, I was able to find references to slaves with likely names associated with Spartanburg. I started clicking through, and now in burning-the-midnight-oil mode, I almost allowed myself to get lazy and skip an entry for a fellow named David Patterson. Fortunately, I resisted the urge, and that's when things started to get inte███████████

The 1850 codicil to Patterson's will mentioned a "girl about six years old named Melvina." Essentially, he was leaving Melvina to his wife to take care of her when he died. Once his wife passed away, Melvina and her "issue and increase"—her children—were to be sold. At this point, I didn't let the meaning of the words sink in because all my energy was focused on finding Melvina, and a little math suggested that this could be the one I was looking for.

Impatiently, I commissioned some research at the Family History Library in Salt Lake City, seeking to obtain a complete set of all the estate-related papers of this David Patterson. When the documents arrived the following evening (not typical—I work with talented people who are kind enough to accommodate my fast-turnaround requests), I digested them. Apparently, Patterson had died just two years later, but it seemed that his wife had predeceased him. This meant that Melvina was mixed in with the rest of his possessions for equal distribution among his children.

I raised an eyebrow as I caught the name Shields in his estate's inventory. One of his daughters, Christianne Shields, inherited Melvina. I jumped online to search through records and trees, and it didn't take long for me to piece together that this daughter had married a Shields and moved from South Carolina to—you guessed it, Clayton County, Georgia—and it was one of her sons, Charles, who was living next to Melvina in the 1870 census that had sparked my search for her. That's when I knew that this was definitely the Melvina I was looking for. I had finally found her!

Mixed Feelings

This would seem to be a moment of victory, and it was, but if you've never done African American genealogy, it's hard to appreciate that this is also a time of warring emotions. On the one hand, you're thrilled to have finally found the person you're looking for. On the other hand, nothing prepares you for the experience of seeing human beings with price tags attached—and that's what happened with Melvina. Michelle Obama's great-great-great-grandmother was valued at $475.

I don't care how much of this research you've done, how many slave ancestors you've traced and whether they're yours or not—seeing people with sticker prices is something you never get used to. But I took solace in knowing that I had finally peeled back the layers to Melvina's early days, and as a result, I could now trace the migration of the Shields family from South Carolina to Georgia to Alabama to Illinois—and on to the White House. Now *that's* a Great Migration.

CHAPTER ELEVEN

The Road to a
First Lady's Roots

*Road-tripping to discover all that's not online
about Michelle Obama's heritage*

WHY WOULD ANYONE BOTHER to conduct research the old-fashioned way anymore? Think about the time and expense involved in traipsing around the state, country, or world to spend days buried in musty archives in the hope of finding one or two little pieces of the puzzle. What a hassle. After all, everything's online now, right? It's all been digitized and transcribed, so you can search from the comfort of your own home and print off the results in just minutes.

Well, not quite. In 2007, the *New York Times* looked into the sudden fervor for digitizing everything under the sun—a trend I am wholeheartedly in support of—and reached an interesting conclusion. At the current rate of digitization, it would take approximately 1,800 years to capture the contents of the National Archives text-based collections. Mind you, this doesn't include all the non-text items—photos, films, and so forth—and speaks solely of the National Archives, so it doesn't address any other repository. So if you don't mind waiting another eighteen centuries, we'll be partway there.

Of course, digitization techniques continually improve. Every year, we can snag more and do so faster than the previous year, so that multi-millennial estimate might sound amusing before long, but even so, what's available at the National Archives—as vast as it might be—is the proverbial tip of the iceberg. Countless insights to our collective past remain hidden in local, under-funded repositories, and even in our sophisticated twenty-first century, the only way to find those treasures is to get in the car or hop on a plane and do some intensive digging.

To give you a sense of what you can unearth with on-site research, I thought I'd take you on the road with me as I explored a portion of Michelle Obama's family history. In the last chapter, I followed her Shields branch, which migrated through a series of four states. In this chapter, I've decided to focus on the part of the country that holds more of her personal history than any other place: Henry and Pittsylvania counties in Virginia, with particular emphasis on the former. Fully a quarter of her ancestry traces to this region. Were she to visit Martinsville, she would be walking among more hidden cousins than anyplace else other than Chicago where the various branches of her family eventually intertwined due to the Great Migration.

It's true that I was able to find the names and approximate birth years of many of her ancestors from this pocket of the country online, but a decent genealogist seeks to get past those basic details. Ideally, you want to get a feel for your ancestors' environment, what they endured, and what they were like as living, breathing people. What follows is a sampling of nuances and insights that could only have been uncovered by hopping in my purple Fit, setting the GPS, and heading south to conduct on-site research in Virginia at the Library of Virginia, Henry County Courthouse, Bassett Historical Center, and the

Virginia-North Carolina Piedmont Genealogical Society, and in Washington, D.C., at the National Archives.

Colored Persons Cohabiting

It's Henry County that produced one of the most intriguing documents I encountered during my research. Many, though not all, of Michelle Obama's ancestors were enslaved and treated as property. Those who have any experience with African American genealogy know well that this harsh reality adds insult to injury because it effectively renders one's ancestors next to invisible. When trying to push back to pre-Emancipation days, it's necessary to identify the slave owner, so the document I'm about to share—the *Register of Colored Persons cohabiting together as Husband and Wife on 27th February, 1866*—is something of a mixed blessing. While it has its origins in the countless indignities of slavery, it is invaluable to those descended from those listed in it.

Shortly after Emancipation, the General Assembly in Virginia passed a law to permit what amounted to a retroactive solemnization of the marriages of former slaves in the state. Previously denied the privilege of marriage, couples could now register their names and those of their children at the local courthouse, and both the marriage and offspring would thereafter be regarded as legitimate in the eyes of the law. Over the last century and a half, many of these lists have disappeared for a variety of reasons, but the registry for Henry County survives, and along with it, precious family details. In fact, this is the first recording of the full names of most of those enumerated in its pages.

Several pairs of Mrs. Obama's ancestors took this opportunity to legitimize their unions, including Peter and Dolly Jumper and their children. What sets them apart from her other predecessors is that they were free long before Emancipation (more on this shortly). This cohabitation list was found in the Local Government

Records Collection of the Library of Virginia in Richmond, but those with Henry County roots are more fortunate still due to the Bassett Historical Center and the efforts of local researchers John B. Harris and Beverly Millner.

Bassett is the home of Bassett Furniture, but most of its factories are quiet now and the Center is a beehive of activity in an otherwise slumbering town. It was here that Harris (sadly, no longer with us) and Millner spent many retirement years carefully recording the history of African Americans in Henry County. Among other endeavors, they transcribed the hard-on-the-eyes cohabitation list. The same Jumper listing is seen here much more clearly than the original, making it easy to absorb the names and ages of all family members. Note the word *free* in the columns for the name of the last owner.

Mrs. Obama's Tinsley ancestors also availed themselves of this opportunity, and from their entry, we learn that Tillman Tinsley was born in Pittsylvania County and once considered the property of James Tinsley, while his wife, Amy, was a Henry County native whose former "mistress" was Mrs. A. Thornton. This raises questions of how they managed a family life of any kind with different owners, but their eight children is evidence that they had done so since 1847, and this situation was not especially unusual.

NAME OF CHILDREN WITH AGE OF EACH	DATE OF COMMENCEMENT OF COHABITATION
1. JOE 5, JACKSON 3, RUSAND 1	1860
2. CYNTHIA 15	1858
3. JENNY 6	1859
4. SERENA 28, JOHN 26, LITHA 17, PUSSY 15, PETER 14, DICK 11, MOLLY 10	1831

An invaluable transcription of the "Register of Colored Persons cohabiting together as Husband and Wife on 27th February, 1866" compiled for Henry County, VA, by John B. Harris. (Bassett Historical Society)

Slaves Serving the Confederacy

Another pair of Mrs. Obama's ancestors, Esau and Amy Wade, is also in this cohabitation list. Esau Wade, a great-great-great-grandfather of hers, was one of her more intriguing ancestors. Born into slavery in the early 1820s, he was crowding his forties when the Civil War began. Although the war undoubtedly affected his life and family in many ways, it had its most direct impact toward the end when a requisition from the Virginia governor mandated the provision of 10 percent of Henry County male slaves between the ages of eighteen and fifty-five.

Documentation I found at the Library of Virginia revealed that Esau was designated to serve the Confederacy. On January 7, 1865, Esau's then owner, John D. Wade, sent him for examination to serve by furnishing labor for public works. I suspect that Esau was particularly fit as he was the oldest man not exempted from duty that day, but it's hard to fathom how he must have felt as he was inspected.

No record of his service has been unearthed so far, so it may be that it remains to be found or that he was able to avoid serving since the war was entering its final stages. But it makes me wonder. Though Virginia Governor Bob McDonnell revised his Confederate History Month proclamation in 2010 to include mention of slavery, how many today remain unaware that many slaves— including perhaps this ancestor of a future First Lady as well as so many others in Henry County today—were obligated to serve the Confederacy?

Proving Your Freedom

I mentioned earlier that Michelle Obama's Jumper ancestors indicated that they had been free before Emancipation. In the columns where others listed the names of their last owner, Peter and Dolly Jumper simply said "free." While this certainly made the Jumpers a distinct minority, many don't know that approximately 10 percent of African Americans were free prior to Emancipation. This is an important reality for anyone interested in African American genealogy because those of us living today had quite a few ancestors back in the 1860s. Depending on your age and assuming generations of roughly twenty-five years, you might have had approximately sixteen, thirty-two, or sixty-four direct-line forebears at the time (two parents, four grandparents, eight great-grandparents, etc.). And with so many branches in your family tree, there's a decent chance that at least one of them was free.

The reason this matters is because those ancestors will be easier to research since they weren't hidden behind the obscurity that slavery inflicted on so many. Free ancestors will appear in census, military, and other records with all the details genealogists hope for—names, dates, and places. Moreover, their paper trail will often be supplemented by regular appearances in local court records. Why? Because they had to prove their freedom—over and over again.

In Virginia, the General Assembly passed an act in 1793 requiring the registration of free blacks. It was only about a decade earlier in 1782 that Virginia had passed an act permitting the manumission of slaves, but the growing number of free blacks during that interval concerned some, so the 1793 legislation was the beginning of ▉▉▉▉▉▉▉▉▉▉controls on the African American population. Free blacks had to register every three years at the local courthouse, and lists were maintained by the courts. Once registered, an individual was given "free papers," which had to be produced on demand to prove one's status.

Although the direct link to Mrs. Obama's family is unclear, the first known recording of a Jumper registering for freedom in Virginia is found in Petersburg in 1800. According to research conducted by Paul Heinegg (author of *Free African Americans of North Carolina, Virginia and South Carolina*), a woman named Hagar Jumper asserted her freedom on the basis of her descent from an Indian woman. His research also referenced earlier mentions of Jumpers dating back to a court case involving Tuscarora Indians in 1707, suggesting that this First Lady may well have some Native American ancestry.

If one follows the path of those bearing the Jumper name in Virginia, a gradual southwestern migration becomes apparent until some reached Henry and Pittsylvania counties where Mrs. Obama's family lived. It's Pittsylvania County where Richard Jumper (probably a brother of her third great-grandfather) registered for freedom in 1838. At the time, he was about twenty years old and five foot ten, and the details provided indicate that he had several scars as well as a sixth finger on each hand.

By the 1850s, records show Mrs. Obama's family in Henry County. Below, for instance, are several members of her family, including her third great-grandmother Dolly, in a list of "free Negros over 12 years" that I found at the local courthouse. Three years later in May 1859, members of the same family returned to the courthouse together to keep their registration in good standing.

This branch of Mrs. Obama's ancestors was fortunate in gaining its freedom earlier than others, but was required on a recurring basis to substantiate and reassert their liberty. To try to

The Jumper family registering their freedom in 1856. (Henry County, VA)

get even the slightest trace of perspective, think for a moment how much you detest going to the motor vehicles office to renew your license every few years. Now imagine that failing to do so could result in your becoming enslaved. That's how much this document mattered, and yet you won't find it in any database.

The last record in which the Jumpers stated their freedom is the 1866 cohabitation list discussed at the outset of this chapter. Some eighty years later in 1946, Margie Jumper—born in Henry County, but then living in Roanoke, Virginia—was arrested for refusing to give up her seat on a bus when a white man who had just boarded asked the conductor to make her get up. This was almost a decade before Rosa Parks would do the same in Montgomery, Alabama. True, Margie had married into the Jumper name, but she certainly lived up to its history that day. And incidentally, I learned about her brave stand from a clipping I found in the Bassett Historical Center.

A Gubernatorial Connection

The 1866 cohabitation list for Henry County included most, but not all, of Mrs. Obama's ancestors who were residing there at the time. For whatever reasons, her Morehead branch is absent from this useful resource, making it considerably more difficult to pick up their trail. This family was headed by the distinctly named Powhatan, so the techniques I used to find Melvina as described in the last chapter would have, under better circumstances, worked. But Powhatan and his family slipped through the cracks. For instance, a relevant estate file that normally would have listed slaves by name mentioned none because the wife of the deceased inherited the entire estate.

Still, I had a clue who might have owned the family because of the name Morehead. In the 1870 census, the first one taken post-Emancipation, there are only three Morehead families in Henry County and all of them are African American. Many believe that one-time slaves took their names from their former owners, but I've seen countless exceptions to this. Even so, it's a good first guess, so I always investigate this possibility.

In this instance, I came up empty. Not only were there no white Moreheads in Henry County in the 1870 census, there were none in 1860 or 1850. But there were a few slave-owning Moreheads just across the border in Rockingham County, North Carolina. In 1860, James T. Morehead owned one slave, James M. Morehead owned one slave, Obedience Morehead owned one slave, and John M. Morehead owned twenty-eight. It didn't take much research to ascertain that they were all members of the same family and that John Motley Morehead, owner of the majority of the slaves, was the former governor of North Carolina. In fact, he is known as "the father of modern North Carolina" (due primarily to his initiatives in education and transportation) and was honored in 1995 for his "great leadership and accomplishments" on the 200th anniversary of his birth by the General Assembly of North Carolina.

The natural assumption would have been that Mrs. Obama's Morehead ancestors had been owned by this one-time governor, but I dug a little deeper and reached a slightly different conclusion: they were owned by Mary Morehead Scales, the governor's sister. Mary married Peter Perkins Scales, who built Thornfield Plantation for his new bride around the late 1820s, making her the only member of the Morehead family to reside in Henry County itself. When her husband died in 1845, she inherited Thornfield, as well as everything and every*one* associated with it.

Powhatan's birth happens to coincide with the construction of Thornfield, both having occurred in around 1825–1830, and the man who was likely his father was born in North Carolina. Stitching all the pieces together, I suspect that Powhatan's immediate family was brought into the Scales household by Mary at the beginning of or early in her marriage. Most of Mary's sixty-plus slaves at the time of Emancipation adopted the Scales name

she married into, but three—George, Ben, and Powhatan (indications are that George may well have been the father of the
other two)—elected Morehead instead. I believe they did so due
to earlier affiliation with the Morehead family of Rockingham
County, a name that would have become somewhat prestigious
due to its gubernatorial connection.

I base this on a series of clues initially scouted out online, but
reinforced by on-the-ground discoveries:

- In addition to being the only Morehead family member
  residing in Henry County from at least 1850 to 1870,
  Mary owned forty slaves in 1850 and sixty in 1860,
  including plenty that mapped with the age and gender
  characteristics of Powhatan's family at the time.

- Rather astonishingly, on-site research revealed that Mary
  had taken the trouble to register the births of some of her
  slaves. By comparing these records to the 1870 census, it
  can be established that she owned George Morehead, the
  fellow believed to be Powhatan's father and the oldest of
  the three to use the Morehead name after the abolition of
  slavery.

- Although the signals are less clear with Powhatan, Mary
  definitely owned a slave named Eliza who bore children in
  the 1850s and 1860s, and Powhatan was married to an
  Eliza who had children during that same time frame.

- Post-Emancipation proximity is frequently an indicator of
  former ownership, and in the 1870 census, Powhatan
  and his family were just one page away from Mary with
  several African American Scales families in between, at
  least two of which were owned by Mary according to the
  cohabitation list. Several other families confirmed to have
  been owned by her lived within a ten-page range in this
  same census, and in the 1880 census, Powhatan is on the
  same page as Mary.

Many of Powhatan and Eliza's descendants later lived in Rockingham County, North Carolina, and it was only when I traveled to the Thornfield Plantation in person that I realized that it was just a short stroll from there across the state line to North Carolina. Moreover, I learned that descendants of Mary's continue to live at Thornfield to this day. Owned by the Scales family even before Peter built the home for Mary back in the 1820s, it is now a National Bicentennial Farm.

What makes Mary an intriguing owner is not just the fact that her home remains in family hands today or that her brother was the "father of modern North Carolina," but also that she left traces that provide an unusual glimpse into how she viewed her slaves. In a letter found at the National Archives (and like so many of its holdings, not available online), she wrote to the Confederate government imploring that her youngest son be exempted from service. Here is a portion of that September 1862 letter (italics mine):

> *My family consists of about seventy persons, the white members of which are my mother 91 years old with a recently broken bone now as helpless as an infant, myself and two invalid daughters and my youngest is son on arriving at the age of 18 years.* My three grown sons are in the Army ... leaving my helpless family to the entire care of my youngest son the subject of this communication. I know my country needs all her children and I had thought I could submit to her requisitions. I have given her cause my prayers, my time, my means and my children, but now the last lamb of the fold is to be taken, the mother and helpless woman triumph over the patriot and I beg at your hands an exemption from the conscription for my last and youngest son Edgar F. Scales. . . . *This is the more necessary as there are more than a thousand slaves in five or six miles of me, several of the plantations*

have neither proprietor nor overseer. Prudence would dictate
that some persons should be left in such localities.

Though she begins the letter including the sixty-five slaves she owned at that time as part of her family, her concluding comments intimate her underlying fear—not necessarily of her own slaves, but of slaves in the vicinity in general. In her attempt to build a case to get her youngest excused from service, she was more candid than most male slave owners would have been, and that candor gives us some insight into life at Thornfield where Michelle Obama's Morehead ancestors toiled.

Online vs. On the Road

In researching the heritage of Mrs. Obama, I could have contented myself with what was available online, and if I had, I would have an impressive collection of names and dates. But I wouldn't know about the Jumpers having to repeatedly prove their freedom, I wouldn't have learned about Esau Wade being inspected to serve the Confederacy, and I wouldn't have imagined that the plantation where her family once served the sister of a governor would still be in the hands of that same family today. I would, in short, be unaware of all the history gently hidden just beneath the surface in Henry County, a mere 260 miles from Washington, D.C.

CHAPTER TWELVE

King of America

*Who would rule America today if
George Washington had been king?*

EVERY ONCE IN A WHILE, I encounter a challenge that makes my brain hurt. Trying to identify the king or queen of America was one such case. Yes, I'm aware that there's no monarchy in the United States, but in the genealogical realm, that's just a technicality.

History buffs will recall that George Washington was once encouraged to assume the crown. Responding to Colonel Lewis Nicola, a Frenchman who had served on the American side and raised the suggestion, Washington retorted, "Let me conjure for you, then, if you have any regard for your Country, concern for yourself or for posterity, or respect for me, to banish these thoughts from your mind and never communicate, as from yourself or any one else, a sentiment of the like nature." In short, he wasn't keen on the idea.

Even so, for those who like to play with historical what-ifs, this is a biggie. Who would be king or queen of America today if Washington had become king?

The Request

I was once innocent of the nuances of royal succession and words like *agnatic*, but that was before the request came from Jen Utley and Jeanie Croasmun, editors of the now regrettably defunct *Ancestry Magazine*. If George Washington had become king, would it be possible to determine who would sit on the American throne today? Well, I could certainly give it a try. So started my education.

I launched my mission with a quick scouting of online lineages. Not surprisingly, there are countless family trees across the Internet that incorporate George Washington. If he's any sort of relative of yours, you're naturally going to make sure he's included, even if the connection is exceedingly distant. So I swiftly found numerous trees. What became apparent almost as quickly is that there's no truly comprehensive Washington genealogy online.

I realized that this would be an issue since I would likely have to explore multiple branches of the family tree to identify—and almost more importantly, eliminate—potential monarch candidates. But before venturing further into the Washington forest, I decided that I needed to address my ignorance of the rules of royal succession.

Agnatic vs. Cognatic

I was so new to this topic that I didn't even know what to google to learn more. I experimented with phrases like "rules of royal descent," which led to terms like *hereditary monarchy*, and eventually to *agnatic* and *cognatic*—words that were completely foreign to me.

At the risk of offending those who grasp all the nuances of royal succession, my interpretation—admittedly an over-simplification—boiled down to a few basics. With *agnatic* primogeniture, the succession is all male, all the time, and birth order plays an important role. With *cognatic* primogeniture (or male-preference primogeniture), females get to play, provided all the usual male suspects have died out. There's also *agnatic-cognatic* (I'm not making this up), which lets females in the picture, but places greater emphasis on consanguinity or proximity of blood than on primogeniture.

I figured that even though the United States had won its freedom from England, we would have most likely patterned ourselves after the model of the United Kingdom—and with Queen Elizabeth on the throne, it was evident that the U.K. allows females in the queue under at least some circumstances. But just when I began to hope that I might be able to wade through all the branches of the Washington tree using a single approach, the next stage of my research indicated that I wasn't going to get off that easy.

Why Reinvent the Wheel?

It occurred to me that others must have addressed this question before, so I wanted to see what the earlier conclusions were. Somewhat to my surprise, I only located three thoughtful considerations of the matter. The most recent, "Stubborn Washington Spurned Kingdom," appeared in *The Washington Times* in July 2000. I discovered that *Life* had published an article entitled "If Washington Had Become King" in February 1951. And finally, a search of Google Books turned up a May 1908 piece called "If Washington Had Been Crowned" in *The Scrap Book*, a periodical I was grateful to have tripped across.

I snagged copies of all three, hoping against hope that they would all reach the same conclusion. I wanted a neon sign pointing to one person, but what I found—through no fault of any of the able writers—was additional confusion. This table summarizes the outcome of each of the articles—all of which crowned an individual, but in some way, included a backup king, which I've dubbed the "safety monarch." It's similar to the "heir and a spare" concept, only in these situations, the spare is attributable to differing succession interpretations and, consequently, can come from a far-flung branch of the family tree.

	FIRST CHOICE	SAFETY MONARCH
1908	Thornton Augustine Washington	William Lanier Washington
1951	Frank Washington Craig	Lawrence Washington
2000	Felix Clark Craig	Paul Emery Washington

I was both appreciative of and befuddled by the groundwork laid for me—appreciative that I now had a running start, but befuddled by the multiple monarchs. The connection between the Craigs was easy enough to see—they were father and son—but even with the sketchy Washington family tree I had started to assemble, the links among the rest were far from obvious.

John A. Washington

I was in need of rescue and found it in the form of John A. Washington, a family member and partner in a Washington, D.C–based investment counsel firm. The article from 2000 stated that the editors had relied heavily on his research and he was liberally quoted throughout. It was also clear that he knew his agnatic from his cognatic, so I was confident that he could help.

It was easy enough to locate Mr. Washington and he graciously agreed to be interviewed. I caught him at the office and was dazzled by his photographic memory of all aspects of the extended Washington clan. In short order, I learned that his research had also served as the basis for the 1951 *Life* article. Now

I was certain I was speaking to the only person who could make everything make sense.

Curious about his intricate knowledge, I asked about how he had first ventured into the complex world of Washington genealogy. He explained that back in the 1940s, while a med student, he had been bedridden with tuberculosis and was advised to have complete rest, meaning he was not to look at his medical books. Resting but restless, he looked for something to occupy his time. "I was always aware of my name and my connection to the old general," he said, "and it occurred to me that it would be interesting to learn more about the family tree. And of course, it turned out to be perfectly gigantic."

How gigantic? By John's estimates, roughly 8,000 relatives— fewer than 150 of them still bearing the Washington name— could factor into the succession equation. Eight thousand? Yikes.

Two Assumptions

If there were potentially as many as 8,000 candidates, I wondered, how had John managed to zero in on those singled out in the 1951 and 2000 articles? Did he, for instance, favor agnatic or cognatic succession? In other words, did he take the all-male approach or did he allow for female candidates? Wisely, he declined to state a preference, and explained that this was one of the reasons for the multiple designees.

I followed this with another question that had been vexing me. George Washington died without issue, so the line of succession would have had to veer right from the start through one of his brothers. But which brother? Would it be his older half brother, Augustine, or his next younger, full brother, Samuel?

In most succession schemes, primogeniture plays a critical part. You start with the oldest male and work your way down the age-chain. Augustine, George, and Samuel all shared the same father, so if the monarchy had started with Dad, Augustine would have had first dibs. George, therefore, never would have gotten his turn at the theoretical kingship. But the scenario I was investigating included a complication that could only exist at the beginning of the line—an older brother. Should I give seniority its due and go to Augustine or should the crown pass, as it usually does, to or through the next oldest? The writers of the earlier articles had shown a gentle preference for Samuel, the younger brother, but hedged their bets by acknowledging that Augustine's descendants might have disagreed. I wasn't sure where I stood, but thought that Augustine's branch should at least be given the chance to play.

John seemed pleased that I had done my homework and pointed out that I was wrestling with the second major assumption that resulted in multiple candidates. The agnatic versus cognatic dilemma was further complicated by the older half brother versus younger full brother conundrum. Depending on your choices, this produced four possible succession paths:

- Agnatic/older half brother
- Agnatic/younger full brother
- Cognatic/older half brother
- Cognatic/younger full brother

This explained all the theoretical monarchs designated in the different articles. I was pleased that I now understood the root of my confusion and resolved to follow in the proud tradition of my predecessors and decide not to decide. I wouldn't play favorites, but instead, would follow all four possible monarchy trails.

The Paul Emery Washington Convergence

Just when I thought I was getting a handle on the situation, John mentioned that two of the four options had converged upon

one man: Paul Emery Washington. Being even lightly acquainted with the Washington tree, I knew that Paul was an unlikely king. He didn't spring from a series of firstborns, but rather,
assorted third and fourth-borns. If he was a contender at all, it
was due to the agnatic, no-girls-allowed mode of succession that
can occasionally toss the crown to the most remote of cousins.

John told me that Paul had bubbled to the top in one path
because the elder half brother's line had daughtered out. If you
exclude females, this line had died out all the way back to
Augustine, George's big brother. He informed me that the last
fellow in this line, William A. Washington, died in 1994, so the
Washington surname had now gone extinct in this particular
branch.

Given that Augustine had been born around 1720, that
seemed like a stretch. I knew that John knew his stuff. I wasn't
second-guessing him, but as a genealogist, I had to see for myself.
It was one thing for me to accept that this branch had died out
after almost three centuries. Most of us are aware that surnames
occasionally wither out. But what truly baffled me is how the
next-in-line to William A. Washington could be Paul Emery
Washington. As far as I could tell, they were from completely different branches of the family tree.

Add to this the assertion that Paul was a double-candidate
due to the passing and daughtering-out of *another* very distant
cousin of his in 1997, and I was skeptical. I was confident that I
would be able to make the connection between Paul and both of
his sonless cousins, but for Paul to be the heir apparent of either
of them (much less both), it seemed that countless Washington
men would have to be eliminated as monarch-candidates
through the generations. I wasn't looking forward to identifying
and de-kinging all those males, but a complete database would
certainly help.

I suspected the answer, but cautiously asked John whether he
might have such a database. No, he had started in the 1940s with
paper and pen, and he continued that way today. There was a

fellow in Florida who had the information in electronic format, but he probably wouldn't appreciate this speculative inquiry.

I had secured several books I thought might help, but none seemed comprehensive enough for the task that lay before me, so I solicited John's advice. He suggested the second edition of *Burke's Presidential Families of the United States of America.* I thanked John for his time and then thanked my lucky stars for online shopping that makes it so easy to purchase a twenty-seven-year-old book.

Wading Through the Washingtons

The book arrived and I started to work my way through all four paths, starting with the easiest one. The cognatic/younger full brother combination that had led in earlier articles to the Craig family was fairly straightforward to follow. George (via his brother Samuel) to his nephew Thornton, to his son John, to his son Lawrence, to his brother Daniel, to his son Thornton, to—allowing for females—his nephew Frank (via his sister Elizabeth), to his son Felix, who was designated in the 2000 article. Follow that?

Felix had passed away in 2002, but it wasn't difficult to identify the next in line, Franklin H. Craig. Consulting the data in *Burke's,* I assured myself that no candidates had been overlooked. Phew! That wasn't too difficult. One down, three to go.

The cognatic/older half brother combination was a little more confusing, particularly due to the 1908 article. As I followed this succession route, I realized that I couldn't account for William Lanier Washington, one of the kings mentioned in this piece. But a close reading revealed that the writer had dismissed a first-son line in the chain because that son "was completely lost sight of by his family, though efforts were made to find him." Since 1908, the Washington clan had managed to pick up his trail, bumping William Lanier Washington out of his former spot.

Instead the line led from the lost son, Bushrod Washington, to his son Spotswood, to his son Bushrod II. At this point, females would have entered the picture because Bushrod II only had a daughter named Estella. Queen Estella would have reigned from 1918 to her death in 1931, but because her only child had predeceased her, the succession would have swung to her oldest uncle's branch. He was also deceased, but had two living children from separate marriages. The son, though younger and from the second marriage, would have been given preference, so that would give America a King Lee from 1931 to 1969. Lee also only had one daughter. Like her father, Queen Odelle would have enjoyed a lengthy rule—1969 to 2000. And with her majesty's passing, we would now be under the dominion of Queen Brynda.

Although I'd like to think I'm neutral in all this, I have to confess that the notion of kings and queens with names like Spotswood, Bushrod, Estella, Lee, Odelle, and Brynda is appealing. And the fact that Odelle married into the Hanson name is even more fitting, given that a gentleman by the name of John Hanson is sometimes referred to as the first president since he was the first President of the United States in Congress Assembled to serve under a fully ratified Articles of Confederation.

Against-the-Odds Paul

So depending on whether you started with Augustine or Samuel, America winds up with Queen Brynda or King Frank II (his grandfather was also Frank). But now it was time to investigate the agnatic, or male-only, lines that supposedly both converged on Paul Emery Washington. I knew I was in for some serious genealogical slogging.

I decided to start with the agnatic/younger full brother combination. This was the same as the cognatic/younger brother path all the way until it reached the second Thornton, who passed away in 1935. Using the strictly all-male approach, there were no

more candidates in his part of the family tree, so it became necessary to back up to Thornton's long-deceased uncle Benjamin and
come forward through his line. This led to Lawrence Washington, one of those enthroned in the 1951 article. Although he
gamely carried the virtual crown for many years, he passed away
in 1997 at the age of ninety-seven.

Lawrence had a daughter, but the agnatic requirement to exclude females forced a retreat back up his line. His father's only
brother had died without issue, so it was back to his grandfather.
Some of his grandfather's brothers' lines already had to die out
for Lawrence to have come into contention in the first place, and
I watched in amazement as more than half a dozen other candidates removed themselves from the monarch pool by dying
young, remaining lifelong bachelors, or marrying but having no
children. So now it was back to Lawrence's great-grandfather.
The same pattern repeated itself with all possible candidates
erasing themselves from consideration.

I eventually found myself all the way back at Samuel, George
Washington's younger full brother. Having already ruled out all
the descendants from his children from his first three wives (he
had five in all), I turned to wife number four. It was his fourth son
by his fourth wife, Lawrence Augustine Washington, who finally
led to a viable line of males. And as the great-great-grandson of
Lawrence Augustine, Paul Emery was indeed the next in line. So
the chain of succession had veered across multiple generations
and branches from Lawrence, who passed away in 1997, all the
way to Paul, his fourth cousin.

Dreading what was to come, I steeled myself for the
agnatic/older half brother trail. Had it also, as John indicated,
died out all the way back to Samuel? I started with William
Augustine who had died in 1994 in his late eighties. I couldn't
help but notice that there seemed to be a recessive gene in the
Washington family that conveyed longevity along with the faux-
monarchy. But in conjunction with those traits, it also seemed to
pass along a predisposition for being the last in the line.

Returning my attention to William Augustine's line, I worked my way back one generation and one branch at a time, ping-ponging between *Burke's* and the software (note to the publisher of *Burke's*: in the future, please consider using a font larger than size three). I found myself softly humming Queen's "Another One Bites the Dust" as I crossed off several for marrying, but having no kids. Numerous bachelors adorned the Washington family tree and I summarily lopped off their stunted branches as I continued my climb. Still others died young.

When I finally got to the top, I saw that I had once again arrived at Samuel. This meant that with the 1994 passing of William Augustine, the agnatic paths for the older half brother and younger full brother had essentially merged, so I knew where this was going. After a brief detour through Lawrence (1994–1997), the crown went once again to Paul. Yes, John was right. Paul Emery was the double winner of the agnatic sweepstakes.

ROYAL CANDIDATES	DESCENT VIA OLDER HALF BROTHER, AUGUSTINE, 1718–1751	DESCENT VIA YOUNGER FULL BROTHER, SAMUEL, 1733–1781
Agnatic Succession: **excludes females**	Paul 3rd great-grand-nephew	Paul 3rd great-grand-nephew
Cognatic Succession: **male-preference,** **but allows females** **in certain, limited** **circumstances**	Brynda 5th great-grand-niece & half 5th great-grand-niece	Franklin "Frank" 5th great-grand-nephew

King Frank II, Queen Brynda I, or King Paul I?

Depending on which mode of succession you favor, there are three possible outcomes, just as John A. Washington has told me. I asked him what he made of all this and he politely pointed out that this whole situation was even more hypothetical than it seemed on the surface. After all, he mused, if the family really had been royal, wouldn't at least some of them have made different choices about their marriages? Wouldn't there have been pressure to pair up with other royals? Speaking about George Washington's refusal to become king, he remarked, "The old boy knew what he was doing in that regard." I couldn't agree more.

CHAPTER THIRTEEN

Skeletons in the Turret
Could DNA reveal the identity of the men of the USS Monitor?

MOST CIVIL WAR BUFFS are well-versed in the demise of the USS *Monitor* on the last day of 1862, and many have visited the museum now dedicated to it in Newport News, Virginia. As the first ironclad warship commissioned by the U.S. Navy and one of the combatants in the first-ever ironclad battle (against the CSS *Virginia*, which most of us know better by its earlier name, the USS *Merrimack*), the *Monitor* continues to fascinate even though it saw less than a year of action. Because it's been so intensively studied, we thought we knew all its secrets, but many were astounded in 2002 when it was raised from the ocean floor and two skeletons were found in the turret.

I love getting out-of-the-blue calls inviting me to play history detective, so I was tickled a few years later when BBC contacted me from London asking whether I could track down the families of any of the sixteen sailors who lost their lives when the *Monitor* went down. The hope? DNA testing to identify remains. Due to

138

my work with the army, this was familiar territory for me. In fact, the same lab would be conducting the genetic tests.

As often happens when I get one of these inquiries, I was told that there wasn't much time. BBC called on Thanksgiving and needed answers by Christmas, so the race was on. While I started with sixteen candidates, the list narrowed rapidly, mostly due to non-genealogical reasons. Isotopic testing on the teeth, for instance, disclosed that both men had ingested water with minerals that indicated they had spent their younger years in Europe. This whittled the possibilities to six, as the other ten were American-born.

As the research progressed and the list grew shorter, all of us became enchanted with a Scottish sailor named James Fenwick. Ultimately, BBC decided to center the show on him, which turned out to be a mixed blessing for me. On the one hand, it allowed me the luxury of concentrating on one sailor, but now I was dealing with an all-our-eggs-in-one-basket situation. What if I couldn't find his family?

Focusing on Fenwick

The Fenwick case was very much like the many others I've looked into for the army since 1999, but with one difference—the time frame. Working directly with the army, the earliest ones I had tackled previously were WWI soldiers. This time I was re-searching a Civil War sailor, and a foreign-born one to boot.

I should also mention that I did this research about five years ago, and in genealogical years, that might as well have been a lifetime ago. Many resources that would have been useful had not been indexed yet, making them all but impenetrable unless I could learn where he was originally from.

Still, it looked promising at the outset as there was more infor-mation available on Fenwick than most of the sailors. This is because he had married shortly before his death, and his widow had applied for a pension—and pension files generate paper and leave a trail with welcome clues. From his enlistment documents and this file, I knew that his name was James R. Fenwick, he was born in Scotland around 1838–1839, he married Mary Ann Duffy in October 1862 while on leave in Boston, and he had a tattoo that read "J.R.F. Dundee." Compared to the others, this was a treasure trove of information! The tattoo, of course, made me wonder whether he might have originally been from Dundee, Scotland, but we couldn't rule out the possibility that it was perhaps the name of a ship he had served on previously.

While this was a good start, it was far from a slam dunk. First, there was no hint whatsoever about his birth family in Scotland, and that was going to be critical in terms of potential DNA testing. Second, his wife didn't appear in the 1870 census or other records that would have made it easy to pick up the family's trail. The reason this was especially disappointing is that she had claimed in the pension application to be pregnant. Whether she lost the baby or was fibbing in the hope of a higher allotment, we'll never know, but when I finally managed to latch on to her, there was no sign of a child—and with that, went any hopes of descendants.

Brandy, You're a Fine Girl . . .

If you're a reader of a certain age, you might remember a song called "*Brandy*" about a barmaid who works in a harbor town "laying whiskey down" and "loves a man who's not around." To me, Mary Ann Duffy, the woman Fenwick married, was the original Brandy. I began to form this opinion when I found the couple's marriage record.

Mary Ann, it turned out, was Irish. She lived in Boston, then a thriving seaport—and whaddya know?—she really worked in a saloon in a part of town that catered to mariners. Sadly, I would eventually learn that she had also died young, succumbing to cholera in her early thirties, but at this point, I was simply thrilled to see that their marriage record included the names of their parents. I knew I couldn't take this information as gospel, as sailors bouncing around the globe back in the 1860s were adventurous types, not necessarily the kind concerned with leaving an accurate paper trail, but it gave me more to go on than I had before.

Incidentally, I also searched birth records for a possible child, but came up empty-handed. It was a later discovery that would cement Mary Ann in my mind as the original Brandy, but for the moment, I was only interested in seeing whether Fenwick's alleged parents' names could help me find him back in Scotland.

Scotland's People

I'm always jealous of people of Scottish heritage because the government of Scotland has created a wonderful website of genealogical records (in case you're curious, it's www.scotlandspeople.gov.uk) and this is immediately where I went with the new details I had. Fenwick's parents were said to be Charles and Elizabeth, so I poked around looking for such a couple. It took just a few minutes to find them in the 1861 census. In fact, they appeared to be the only Fenwick family in all of Scotland headed by a Charles and Elizabeth. Better yet, Charles was a ship's joiner, a likely profession for the father of a sailor, and he and Elizabeth were of appropriate ages to have been James's parents. There was just one problem: no James.

I reasoned that James would have been old enough to have already been at sea, but this didn't help me as I needed to be able to prove that he was their child. More pounding of databases turned up the 1834 marriage of Charles and Elizabeth. That was good news as it meant that they were married in time to have been his parents. As I pieced together the rest of their family, I also found that there was a convenient gap in children in which

James could have handily fit, but that was hardly proof. Regrettably, there was no birth record for James that would make the connection for me. Government-based birth registers weren't kept until 1855, so I was dependent on church records for a birth in the late 1830s, and that's always a hit-and-miss prospect. I missed.

Seeing that Charles and Elizabeth had a large family of at least eleven children, I calculated that they would have lots of descendants by now, so went looking for online family trees. Perhaps someone else had already linked James to this family. I was half-right. They did have plenty of descendants, now scattered everywhere from Canada to Australia, and many of them were avidly researching them, but *none* of them had a James in the family. Even though this discouraged me, I took some time to bang out e-mails to those who had posted the trees. You never know. It could be useful to compare notes.

Tick-Tock

So now what? I had a family that looked like a perfect fit, but no sign of James. Others who been investigating the family for years also had no James. Could it be possible that they all had incomplete trees, or had James lied about his parents in his Boston marriage record? Was I looking at the wrong family entirely? BBC was going to DNA test people based on my research, and the project was of some historical importance. I couldn't just make a leap of faith and tell the producers that I thought James *probably* belonged to this family.

Skilled genealogists would realize that the logical next step for me was to search earlier census records. Perhaps I could find James with his family in 1841 or 1851. But back in the dark ages of half a decade ago, this was a daunting prospect. While digitized and indexed versions of these records are now available online, they weren't at the time. Worse yet, I was in the peculiar position of knowing that they would be available by the following April, but BBC—which was by now politely clearing its throat and pointing to its watch—needed to film in January.

Before these records were indexed, the way to search them was by location, but rather annoyingly, the confirmed children of Charles and Elizabeth were born all over the place. I got the impression that Charles, as a ship's carpenter, was following building jobs and moving his family wherever they happened to be. It would have helped if any of their numerous offspring had had the consideration to be born in a census year as that would have at least given me a clue where to look, but no such luck. They stubbornly refused to be born in years ending with -1, the years that censuses were conducted in England and Scotland.

The Tide Begins to Turn

Whenever I get stonewalled, I heed Julie Andrews's "Do-Re-Mi" advice and "start at the very beginning" to see what I could have possibly missed. Taking another look at all the documents I had gathered, I registered the name of the clergyman who had performed Fenwick's marriage to Mary Ann Duffy. A little googling told me that Rev. Edward T. Taylor was known as the "Sailor Preacher." He founded the Boston Port and Seamen's Aid Society, which among other things, established the Mariner's House, a boardinghouse where sailors could stay without fear of getting ripped off.

Rev. Taylor was interesting in his own right, and as I delved into his story, I learned that his papers were held at the Massachusetts Historical Society. Hope springs eternal, so I was still nurturing a thought that there could have been a child (perhaps Mary Ann had put the child in an orphanage since she didn't have the means to support a baby on her own). But even if that wasn't the case, maybe the reverend's record of the marriage would include more details, or at least confirm the names of

Fenwick's parents. Time was short, so I hired a local researcher named Ellen Yee and asked her to have a look.

Sure enough, she found the marriage, but no fresh tidbits emerged, and there was still no sign of a child. But she did find something else. Included in the collection were the registration books for the Mariner's House, and there in 1861, was an entry for James R. Fenwick. A notation said that his bill had been paid by his captain. Why, you may wonder, was this fellow picking up his tab? Fenwick had arrived in Boston by virtue of a shipwreck.

Now I understood how a sailor from Scotland had met Mary Ann in Boston. The lyrics of "Brandy" sprang immediately to mind: "Brandy used to watch his eyes when he told his sailor's story. She could feel the ocean fall and rise, she saw its raging glory." Fresh from a disaster at sea, Fenwick had arrived with one heck of a yarn to spin. I also understood why, if this was the man I was seeking, he wasn't with his family in the 1861 census in Scotland. He was too busy being shipwrecked on the other side of the Atlantic.

Poor Fenwick crashed onto America's shores, fell in love, and probably signed on to the USS *Monitor* to remain in the United States with Mary Ann—only to lose his life the following year. What floored me is that this was new information. With more than 60,000 books on the Civil War and ironclads being a popular topic, I didn't expect there to be much left to discover, but I was wrong. Though the men who went down in the *Monitor* have been well-studied, Fenwick's sad journey was a revelation.

Saved by the Two Amelias

True, I was no closer to finding Fenwick's birth family, but this unexpected bonus reinvigorated my flagging spirits, and just about the same time, I got another jolt. As mentioned earlier, I e-mailed a number of Fenwick descendants in several countries. All along, I had continued my correspondence with them, hoping for a break. While there was still no trace of James, I received a message that grabbed my attention because it included a second Amelia.

Everyone I had been communicating with attributed a daughter named Amelia to Charles and Elizabeth. She was the baby of the family, born in 1860. This virtual pen pal had this Amelia, plus another who had died in 1853. I wasn't all that surprised as our ancestors liked to recycle names. Infant and child mortality was once so high that if you wanted a name to persist in the family, you might have to use it several times. That's likely what happened here.

I wondered where she might have found this detail that had escaped everyone else's notice, so I sent her a reply, but in my impatience, immediately started scouring the Internet. That's how I found the Scottish cemetery transcription that had to have been her source. It noted that her father was Charles, a ship joiner. Well, that certainly fit. She had died in Arbroath on October 29, 1853, at the age of eighteen months. How sad, I thought, before selfishly realizing that this meant she had probably been born in early 1852 —as in, just on the cusp of a census year.

Deadline-driven genealogy forces you to be very matter-of-fact about the hardships our ancestors confronted. BBC needed to begin taping soon, and I still hadn't nailed down Fenwick's family. Could this be the clue I needed to find the family in the 1851 census? I consulted the 1861 one I already had, and my hopes sank when I saw that none of the other children had been born in Arbroath. Maybe this Amelia was from another family. But at this point, I had nothing to lose. Why not scroll through the 1851 census for Arbroath? It couldn't be more than a roll or two of microfilm, and maybe not even that much.

I sighed with relief when I finally spied thirteen-year-old James R. Fenwick, already a factory worker in the shipping industry, living with his parents, Charles and Elizabeth, and all the siblings I would have anticipated finding. His birthplace was given as Dundee, answering the question I had about his tattoo.

Just in the nick of time, I had the proof that had eluded me. Now I could tell BBC with confidence that I had identified Fenwick's family.

Not Quite Done

From here on, this case became all about the Amelias. It was all well and good that I was sure of Fenwick's birth family, but BBC needed at least one living relative—preferably one who shared the same maternal DNA. The second Amelia was the youngest in the family, so I decided to start with her and trace her line forward in time. Luck was on my side as this family clearly intended to keep both the Amelia and Fenwick names alive!

Amelia Laing Fenwick, James's youngest sister, was born in 1860. She married and had a daughter named Amelia Fenwick Fraser. This Amelia married and had a daughter named Amelia Fenwick McMorran. And this Amelia, born in 1920, was a terribly good sport and gamely agreed to swab for history's sake and BBC's cameras.

I had the pleasure of chatting with Amelia III since the producers asked me to appear in the documentary as well. I had been hired purely to do the research, but they were so amused with the *sturm und drang* of my e-mails as I updated them on my quest that they thought it might be entertaining to include me. So it was that Amelia and I spoke to each other as camera crews in both of our houses on opposite sides of the Atlantic captured our conversation. A great-niece of Fenwick's, she was aware of a relative who had gone off to America, but this was the first that anyone learned what had become of him. She had no idea that she was related to an American naval hero.

Maybe Yes, Maybe No

You're probably wondering what the genetic verdict was, right? After all this, it was a definite maybe. Mitochondrial DNA is sometimes less precise than we'd like, and particularly with degraded remains, it's tricky business. Amelia's DNA sample did indeed match that taken from one of the skeletons, but the scientists wisely refused to declare victory. You might be perplexed to hear that I'm glad of that. While it certainly would have made for more of a ta-da! ending for the show, the genetic overlap between the two subjects is a relatively common one shared by many others, so it's not possible to rule out good, old-fashioned coincidence.

Scientists working on another history mystery involving an entirely different documentary and set of producers allowed themselves to be swayed by the desire for a tidy ending, only to learn several years later that they were wrong. These geneticists took a better-safe-than-sorry tact, and that's the right way to go. And I have every confidence that advancements in DNA extraction and testing will continue to progress so that we will one day know for sure whether one of the skeletons in the turret was James R. Fenwick, survivor of one, but regrettably not two, shipwrecks.

CHAPTER FOURTEEN

Anatomy of an Adoption Search

Helping adoptees discover who they are

I DEBATED WHETHER to include a chapter on adoption because I don't consider myself an expert in this area, but even so, I've been involved a number of cases—and more to the point, I'm aiming in this book to give as full a picture of genealogy as possible. And there's no denying that adoption affects many families, and genealogy often plays a pivotal role.

I'm not adopted and haven't adopted any children, so I can't pretend to truly understand what it's like to wear those shoes. But that doesn't stop me from having opinions. You probably won't be astonished to hear that I have a bias toward openness. Simply put, I believe that everyone has the right to know who they are. Yes, I could make all the usual, reasoned arguments about the importance of having access to one's medical history and all that, but knowing who you are is at the heart of genealogy, and I can't imagine denying that right to anyone.

That's why I occasionally help. Let me be clear about this. In spite of my views, I don't proactively seek adoption cases and I'm not a campaigner for adoptees' rights. In fact, this is the first time I'm publicly sharing the fact that I've quietly assisted in a number of cases over the years. But when an adoptee somehow trips into my life and requests my aid, I often do what I can. Perhaps I should also mention that I have never accepted payment, which makes me what many refer to as an "adoption angel."

A Few Observations

Based on my experience as a sporadic participant in adoption situations, I've reached several fundamental conclusions:

- Non-identifying information is critical, but once obtained, finding the missing family members is often remarkably easy.
- The process is delicate, so you have to take it slowly.
- The outcome isn't always the "Kumbaya" reunion many imagine.

Adoption.com defines non-identifying information as "health and other family background information which is commonly exchanged or otherwise made available to the other members of the adoption triad, but which does not include identifying information, such as names, addresses, birth dates and telephone numbers." Adoption is regulated state by state, so legally available details vary widely, and as I've discovered, even adoptees from the same state (or same family) may often be given more or less information than others. But going through whatever the process might be in the state of birth to obtain non-identifying information is an essential first step.

Since I'm not an adoption counselor, most who approach me have already done this, but gotten stuck there. What surprises me is how often I'm able to help people at this stage in just a day or two. As a hybrid genealogist-detective who's equally skilled at finding the living and the long-departed, I treat adoption cases no differently from those I do for the army, coroners, NCIS, TV shows, and other purposes—and that approach seems to work.

The downside of speedy success is that the adoptee who made the request isn't always ready for it. Disappointed from past failed attempts to find the birth mother, father, or siblings, he or she has often built up a bit of a protective wall to keep expectations in check, so it can come as a shock when I come skipping back with an address and phone number the next day. Consequently, while it might seem like good news that I've found the missing relative(s), I also try to keep my own expectations in check. I simply share the data gathered and step back. It's up to the adoptee what, if anything, to do with that information.

In most cases, the story moves on to the next chapter—a reunion or contact with one or more family members—but at a pace that can seem slow to those not emotionally invested. For the adoptee, so much is at stake that it takes a lot of guts to make that first contact, so it's not unusual for there to be a let-me-absorb-this period.

That leads to my final observation: it's not always the all-smiles reunions you see on TV. I remember an adoption show from a few years ago where the participants were made to hike up a hill in order to meet their birth mother or other relative. All of this was done on camera, and the host—an adoptee himself—was sometimes in tears even when those being reunited weren't. I've worked on enough television shows to understand the intention, but it struck me as a touch contrived, and well . . . a little unfair. The moment of reunion is stressful enough without a breathless climb, a weepy host, and the pressure of an audience waiting to cheer for that first-hug close-up.

Because of this, I try my best to be a neutral third party. Am I quietly hoping for a happy reunion resulting in an ongoing relationship? Absolutely. But I keep that to myself. While I ask to be kept in the loop, I'm prepared for that not to happen or to not hear anything for quite some time. It may sound paradoxical, but I think I'm able to be of greatest service when I'm willing to assume the role of a detached outsider.

Who I Help

As I mentioned previously, I don't go out seeking adoption cases, but they seem to find me. And incidentally, I define *adoption* more broadly than most. While I assist a number of people who have been formally adopted, I also help others with absentee fathers find them (no mothers so far, but I imagine the day will come). To me, these are like adoption cases in which the adoptee has already obtained non-identifying information. Though there may not have been a formal adoption, and the individual may have been raised by their birth mother, the difficulties of finding the other parent and the ramifications of making contact are similar.

Normally, I become involved almost by accident. For instance:

- I'm doing genealogy consultations on a cruise ship and a septuagenarian adoptee requests my help locating her father's family. (She assumed he had passed away, and was right, but he had lived into his nineties, so she had barely missed meeting him.)

- I'm appearing on a morning show and the producer whispers that she's looking for her birth father and wonders whether I can find him (in that instance, I did so literally overnight in my hotel room).

- Or as with the case I'm about to share, I'm at the gym where someone overhears that I'm a genealogist and asks for my help.

The variety of ways in which I'm pulled into cases underscores just how many lives are touched by adoption.

Case in Progress

It may seem like an odd choice, but I've decided to walk through a case that's still very much in progress. Living birth siblings have been found, as has the (deceased) birth father, though there's a hiccup with regard to him. And the birth mother remains to be found. In the interest of privacy, I've changed names and a few other details, but this midstream case is an ideal one for illustrating both the easy gains and pitfalls that can be involved in the search itself. But fear not, lovers of happy endings, there's a reunion along the way!

I've been going to the same gym and working out with the same trainer for perhaps four or five years now. In all that time, I have never met Monica—had never so much as laid eyes on her—and that's strange because she's also been going to the same gym for years. For whatever reasons, she happened to be there on this one day. My trainer, Pete, knows what I do for a living and told me that another client had been talking about family history, so he mentioned me. He had her contact info on a card and asked me to call her.

As Pete and I chatted, Monica heard our conversation. Giving me a much-welcomed chance to catch my breath, she told me that she was interested in genealogy because she was adopted. I immediately explained to her that I wasn't a trained adoption counselor, so was hesitant to discuss it with her, but asked what, if anything, she knew about her birth family. That's when I learned that she had already taken the initial steps and obtained non-identifying information.

What Monica Knew

Monica knew her birth name, date, and place of birth, and that she supposedly had two older sisters who had been adopted together. This was an excellent start, though she had no clue about her parents' names. I asked what her original surname was, hoping that it wouldn't be Smith or Jones. It turned out to be one of those names that's not too common and not too rare, and that gave me a glimmer of hope. For privacy's sake, I'll say it was Randall.

My next question was her age. Monica wasn't shy and told me her exact birth date, which put her in her early sixties. Though she looked younger, I couldn't help wincing and telling her I wished that she were older. That's because she had been born in New Jersey, and being familiar with accessibility of records in this state, I knew that I might have been able to pluck out her parents' marriage record at the state archives in Trenton if she had been perhaps five to seven years older. Doing some quick math based on her age and the belief that she was the youngest of three, I calculated that her parents had probably married around the mid-1940s, but records are only available for open searching at the archives up to 1940. In general, aging works in adoptees' favor as privacy laws usually have time limits attached. That's the case for Monica as the relevant restriction is fifty years, but post-1940, it's necessary to write to a different New Jersey department for the record—and while I would have been willing to wade through all the Randall entries in the relevant county at the archives, there was no way this department would! Without the names of her birth parents, then, this was a dead end—typical of the catch-22 situations adoptees frequently confront in attempting to obtain records that could be useful for their quest.

So much for a swift solution. Warning Monica to keep her expectations low, I asked her to summarize what she knew in an e-mail, and told her I'd scope out the situation to see if I could find any other ways forward.

Sister-Seeking

Monica didn't waste any time as a lengthy e-mail showed up in my inbox that evening. The message mostly reiterated what she had already told me, but added a few tidbits, such as the fact that her parents were said to be in the midst of divorcing when she was born. As a genealogist, I tend to hit websites like Ancestry.com, FamilySearch.org, and GenealogyBank.com before I even google, but in Monica's case, nothing in particular jumped out, so I decided to "work" Google. I tried a variety of searches, but the magic combination was Randall and the county of birth. Lo and behold, there was an entry for a female Randall born in the same county just three years before Monica. Better yet, it was a recent addition to an adoption registry where people post looking for birth relatives.

The logical assumption was that this might be one of Monica's older sisters. At that point, I could have attempted contact through the registry, but didn't think it appropriate to insert myself into the communication. Instead, I copied the information and sent it to Monica, who was astounded. She had also done some googling, but come up empty. Something as simple as including the county in the search is what made the difference.

I sat back and prepared to wait for a spell, but now it was my time to be caught off guard. Monica, evidently not the type to let grass grow under her feet, made contact almost immediately. Roughly twenty-four hours after I met her in the gym, she e-mailed to tell me about her first conversations with her birth sisters. She had queried the adoption registry and received the details for the one who posted, and called without hesitation. It was just as she had been told. There were two older sisters who had been adopted together, and she spoke with both by phone.

The only catch in all this? Monica's sisters had never known of her existence. Yes, they were older, but just barely, so they had no recollection of their parents and early years. Monica had exercised her rights for non-identifying information and been told about the sisters, but not given her parents' names. The sisters, exercising those same rights in the same state, had been given their parents' names, but not been told about their younger sister. This, too, is typical of what adoptees experience.

This Jack Sprat situation in which her sisters had complementary information meant that Monica now had the names of her parents! Just two short weeks after finding them, Monica went to meet her newfound siblings in person, and I'm happy to report that even though they had had no inkling of her existence, she was welcomed with open arms. So thrilled was she that she repeatedly asked me what she could do to thank me, even offering to pick up my dry-cleaning! Though tempted, I declined her kind offer and asked what her sisters knew about her birth parents. That's when things got confusing.

Things That Make You Go Hmmm...

The sisters told Monica that their parents were Thomas Henry and Beth Randall. Rather inconveniently, no middle or maiden name had been given for their mother, making her difficult to find, but the counselor who had helped the sisters secure the non-identifying information had also informed them that their father passed away in 2006. But I wasn't so sure.

Before traveling to the family reunion, Monica had shared the parents' names with me. Naturally, I had done some searching. I also quickly found the Thomas Randall who had died in the same location the sisters were born. This was the fellow who died in 2006, and since he was of an appropriate age to have been the father and seemingly in the right place, it was a logical conclusion that he was indeed their father.

But as a genealogist, I know how easy it is to be fooled, even with names that sound rare, so I dug deeper. I searched the Social Security Death Index for Thomas Randalls of a likely age (born in the 1920s) whose Social Security had been issued in New Jersey (online databases allow you to be specific if you know how to play with them), and a second candidate emerged. He had passed away several decades earlier in Kentucky, so it appeared to be a long shot, but I couldn't help but notice that military records I checked for him showed that his middle name was Henry. This discovery led me to reinvestigate the one who had died in New Jersey in 2006. While I couldn't find his middle name, records I found gave his middle initial as G. Hmmm...

I needed to break the tie, so decided to order the Social Security application forms for both. (In case you're wondering, these are only available for deceased individuals.) I figured that this would give me the New Jersey candidate's full middle name. I was also aware that the document would give me the address of the Kentucky contender at the time he applied. While I already knew that he was living in New Jersey then, I was curious exactly where. Would it be close to where the sisters had been born or at the other end of the state? That would be telling.

By the time Monica returned from her reunion, I had the answers. The New Jersey fellow's middle name was Garrett, and the Kentucky fellow had lived—you guessed it—about two miles away from where the trio of girls would be born a few years later. In other words, the Thomas Randall who had died in Kentucky back in the 1970s seemed like a better fit for the father.

I explained to Monica that unless her sisters had been misinformed about their father's middle name (a possibility that had to be considered), I believed that they might have the wrong Thomas Randall. Moreover, I had done additional research on the man I thought might really be their father and determined that a second wife of his had passed away, but it appeared that they had a daughter. This meant that there might be another half sister out there. And if she were interested, DNA testing could be used—

provided this possible half sister would agree—to determine for sure whether the Kentucky Thomas was their birth father. (Incidentally, DNA testing has opened new doors for male adoptees for the past several years and a new type—the kind explored in Chapter 20, "Grandma Stepped Out"—has recently provided possibilities for females, so genetic testing will gradually alter the current adoption search process.)

I knew this was a lot to digest, especially on the heels of meeting her sisters so abruptly after six decades, but Monica seemed keen to move forward. At first. Then she slammed on the brakes, and I don't blame her. She was still getting used to having sisters and didn't want to do anything that might disturb their nascent relationship, so was reluctant to raise the father issue with them. It's a bit of an eggshell situation that many adoptees encounter. Once you finally find your birth family, you don't want to risk chasing them away. This was about a month ago, and that's where things stand. And that's where they'll stay unless and until I get a call from her saying that she wants to push on.

Missing Mother

Call it a maternal longing or whatever you wish, but even though Monica has put a hold on learning more about her father, she and her sisters all want to find out who their mother is or was. This is where Murphy's Law steps in to make things difficult. All we have is her first name, Beth. We know she was a Randall at one point, but there's no sign of any such person.

I considered the options and decided to write for a divorce decree. The legally mandated time had passed so the record would be available—provided it could be located—but the search came back "not found" even though more than a decade had been combed through. Most likely, this means that they divorced elsewhere, but it would necessitate a time-consuming, county-by-county quest to try to find out where.

What about a marriage record then? Well, I've written for that as well, but such requests typically take several months to fulfill in New Jersey, and if they married in any other county than the one where the sisters were all born, it's back to square one. With some luck, we'll have Beth's maiden name in a while, but until then, it's a waiting game.

Of course, there are other approaches that could be taken. County court records have already been searched (nada). Newspapers could be scanned for engagement or wedding announcements, but with a period of several years and no indexes, that would be a considerable effort with no guarantee of success. City directories might give an address or narrow the time frame of the marriage, but they're not likely to provide much more than that. If the assumption is made that Beth was local, both the 1930 census and Social Security Death Index could be queried for Beths from that area born in the 1920s, but Beth isn't the rarest of names, so this tactic produces quite a long list of possibilities to have to methodically research one at a time. And if Monica desires, she could also go into private-investigator mode and canvas the area (using addresses obtained from city directories) for elderly residents who might remember her parents. All of these are potential ways to move ahead, but none of them is as promising as the marriage record, so we're waiting and hoping.

To Be Continued

Monica's sisters were found with astonishing speed. Her father is one of two men, but will remain in to-be-determined status unless Monica decides to soldier on (frankly, if she does, I'm rooting for the Kentucky fellow, if only because there's someone living who might have photos or more information to share about him, regrettably not the case with the other one). And if the adoption and genealogical gods are smiling, we might just get traction on her mother in another couple of months. Will this result in another family reunion? I've decided to take it as a positive omen that a quick break to check e-mails just now led me to an article about a sixty-eight-year-old adoptee who recently found and met her 100-year-old mother!

Postscript

The marriage record eventually arrived loaded with helpful information, so I was able to trace the maternal side of Monica's family. Her birth mother passed away about five years ago, but she's had the pleasure of meeting her elderly uncle and some cousins. Both she and her sisters are thrilled to find this uncle, who recalls snippets of their early years. He also told them that their mother had agonized over the decision to give them up, but she had been persuaded that it was for the best. And their birth father? My concerns were justified. He was indeed the fellow from Kentucky.

CHAPTER FIFTEEN

The Slave Who Rescued Freedom

Rediscovering Philip Reed, without whom the Capitol would look very different

IN JANUARY 2009, a man who had vanished into the mists of history made a brief reappearance with the historic inauguration of Barack Obama. The man was Philip "Reid," and if you google his name along with Obama's, you'll find dozens of articles that share the little-known history of Reid, the former slave who made it possible to erect the statue of Freedom that remains on the top of the Capitol dome today. The year was 1863 and Reid had only gained his freedom (by virtue of the D.C. Emancipation Act) on April 16th of the previous year.

Only his name wasn't Reid; it was Reed. That might seem like a minor detail, but Reid is how his owner, Clark Mills, spelled his name. Reed—as in *freed*—is how he himself spelled it, and when you accomplish something of that magnitude, something that is still noteworthy almost a century and a half later, you deserve to have your name recorded correctly. You also deserve to have your story told, so I decided to see what I could learn about Philip Reed's life.

The Slaves Who Built the Capitol

I confess that I had never heard of Philip Reed until shortly before the inauguration. In the weeks leading up to that momentous day, I received quite a few calls from members of the media looking for roots-oriented stories, but one of them in particular caught my attention. Could I learn anything about the slaves who had built much of the Capitol? That seemed tough or almost impossible since much of the construction was done in the early 1800s and I only had days available for research.

But as I explored the topic online, I quickly came across multiple references to Philip Reid. Reid, the accounts said, was a slave who worked for Clark Mills as a skilled plasterer in the 1850s and 1860s. Mills's D.C.-based foundry was given the challenge of casting the statue of Freedom from the plaster model of the sculptor, Thomas Crawford.

The design had been modified from an original version that had the statue wearing a liberty cap. Jefferson Davis, then secretary of war and a slaveholder, objected. The liberty cap had been adopted as the "badge of a freed slave"—and given that he was soon to become president of the Confederacy, it's not surprising that this didn't sit well with him. He requested that the cap be changed to a helmet and it was.

In 1859, an Italian craftsman, thinking he was the only person in America with the necessary skills to oversee a critical and delicate stage in the creation of the statue, hiked his price. Mills refused to capitulate to the demand, and in an irony that escapes few today, turned to his slave Philip Reid to puzzle out how to safely separate the sections of the plaster model and cast them in bronze, producing a statue that would stand almost twenty feet tall and weigh about 15,000 pounds. So it was that a slave rescued the statue of Freedom.

Philip's Story

While there are quite a few references to "Philip Reid" online, I was mystified to find that his story seemed to end with the installation of the statue. What had happened to him afterward? I wondered. Though the media outlet that had initially inquired demonstrated only limited interest, I was curious, so I decided to continue on my own.

The website of the United States Capitol Historical Society told more of the story, showing documents from the National Archives (NARA) and Library of Congress that reveal how we know of Philip's contribution. From NARA was a petition for payment that Clark Mills submitted in which he valued Philip Reid at $1,500 (though many believe that slaves didn't have surnames before Emancipation, some—like Philip—did) and described him as "smart in mind, a good workman in a foundry."

When I later acquired copies of parts of this file not on the website, I found that Mills had gone on to explain that he had purchased Philip as "quite a youth" in Charleston, South Carolina, "because of his evident talent for the foundry business."

The same act that had emancipated Reed also entitled his owner to compensation, and Mills was trying to make his case. While reimbursement for freed slaves was usually limited to $300, Philip was brought back for a second examination and valued at $800.

Under select circumstances, slaves could be paid, and another document shows that "Reid" received $41.25 for dangerous work—"keeping up fires under the moulds"—he performed on thirty-three Sundays between July 1860 and May 1861. Reed's "X" shows that he was given the money on June 6, 1862—roughly seven weeks after he obtained his freedom and almost eighteen months before the statue was put in place. Some articles that mention "Reid" speculate about whether he would have been there on December 2nd when Freedom was erected. Based on what I ultimately learned of him, I'd say so. In fact, he was even buried within sight of his beloved Capitol, but I'm getting ahead of myself.

A Little More on Clark Mills

Because his name was slightly distinctive, I took some time to learn about Clark Mills, and discovered that he was a well-respected artist and sculptor. A New Yorker by birth, he had moved to Charleston, South Carolina, where he married in 1837. In 1850, he owned one slave, a nine-year-old boy, but sometime during the 1850s, he moved to Washington, D.C., where the 1860 slave schedule showed him owning nine slaves. By the time Mills made his claim for compensation in 1862, he owned eleven slaves—Lettie Howard and her six children, an older couple named Thomas, a forty-eight-year-old named Ann Ross, and Philip Reid, listed as forty-two years old. This, then, was an indication that Philip was born around 1820.

Another interesting file emerged in a later claim Mills made in 1864. Restitution could only be made to those loyal to the Union, but a letter purporting to be from Clark Mills, dated December 7, 1861 and sent from D.C., was found in the "Rebel" files of South Carolina. In the letter, he expressed his devotion to his adopted state of South Carolina and proposed setting aside his "favorite art" to make cannons for the Confederacy. The letter was analyzed and deemed to be a forgery, so his claim was spared from rejection. The incident was dismissed and not widely known. When Mills eventually died in January 1883, the *Washington Post* made no mention of it in his obituary, and described his funeral as "very simple, characteristic of the personal life of the great artist, over whose clay they took place."

From Reid to Reed

Now I turned my attention to the man I thought at the time was named Reid, and the obvious first step in my quest was the 1870 census, the first census in which formerly enslaved people are recorded as individuals with names, rather than, say, as an anonymous thirty-seven-year-old male owned by so-and-so. I started with the assumption that Philip had probably stayed local. He was skilled in an unusual occupation and Washington, D.C., seemed as likely a place as any to ply his trade.

He popped up quickly, but not without a few surprises. He was listed as Philip Reed, age fifty, a married, black plasterer, born in Scotland to parents of possibly foreign birth. And he was unable to read or write. With him were what appeared to be his wife and son (the 1870 census doesn't state relationships, though they can often be inferred) and a pair of twentysomethings—perhaps relatives.

Though the birth place of Scotland made me do a double take, I can think of several possible explanations, the most likely being that someone jotted "SC" for South Carolina, but the abbreviation was later interpreted as Scotland. At this point, I hadn't yet discovered the earlier mentioned documents that pointed to South Carolina, but I reasoned that he was probably from this state, since it was unlikely that he would have been able to acquire such specialized skills so quickly unless he had resided with Mills before his move to the District of Columbia.

The 1880 census bore that suspicion out when it gave South Carolina as his birth place, but his son and wife from the previous census were gone and replaced by a new wife, Mary P. I tried to look for his son from the first marriage in the hope of locating descendants, but no promising candidates were found in the 1880 census, so I returned my attention to Philip.

Philip failed to appear in the 1900 census, so I figured that he had died between 1880 and 1900, but what struck me about the census records I had found is that—though he was illiterate—his name was spelled "Reed" each time. This spelling was consistently found in every post-Emancipation document I was to uncover, so that seems to have been his preference.

Philip's Life

Trying to fill in some of the gaps between census records, I quickly found his first marriage—at least his first in Washington, D.C. I can't rule out the possibility that he had a wife and children in South Carolina. The year 1862 was a watershed year for Philip. Mere weeks after gaining his freedom, he got married on June 3, 1862, to Jane Brown. Now I understood why just three days later on June 6th, he sought payment for all those Sundays he had worked back in 1860–1861. He was taking steps to provide a solid start for life with his new bride.

Another marriage record stated that he wed his second wife, Mary P. Marshall, in January 1879. Sadly, the couple would lose a baby girl in 1884. Aside from these events in Philip's life, the paper trail was light, except for city directory entries showing him at various addresses, mostly in southwest D.C., up through 1891.

What Happened to Philip Reed?

I had narrowed the time frame in which Philip died to 1891–1900, and since he didn't appear in later directories, I estimated that he passed away in the early 1890s. A search of Washington, D.C., death certificates confirmed that he had died on February 6, 1892. Yet again, it was easy to see that this was indeed the right man as he was a plasterer born in South Carolina. According to the certificate, he had been a resident of Washington, D.C., since approximately 1857.

The certificate, though, left me with one last mystery: where was he today? I looked for the burial place on the certificate and found it a little difficult to make out due to some scribbled notes. Eventually, I was able to determine that it states that he was buried on the 8th of February in Graceland Cemetery, but "Graceland" was later crossed out and a remark saying, "To Harmony June 21, 1895" had been squeezed in.

I'm a former Washingtonian, but no longer live there today. Fortunately, my sister—well accustomed to my unusual history mystery requests—recently moved back to the area. Stacy went on the trail, though I didn't realize at the time that I was sending her on what would amount to a scavenger hunt. What she discovered is that Philip Reed was initially buried within sight of the Capitol. According to Google Maps, the cemetery was located 1.68 miles away, and standing at the fence that now guards that property, you can easily see the Capitol dome topped by the statue of Freedom.

Curious as to the reason for his removal, I did a bit more research and learned that on August 3, 1894, an act of Congress

Philip Reed was initially buried at Graceland Cemetery within sight of the Capitol. (Stacy Neuberger)

was passed and approved by the president to prohibit any further burials in Graceland and to arrange for the transfer of any bodies already interred there. That's what provoked Reed's reburial at Harmony Cemetery, also known as Harmonia Burial Grounds and Columbian Harmony Cemetery, in 1895. That put him 3.04 miles from the Capitol.

And there he remained until 1959, when Louis and Richard Bell were contracted by the D.C. government to move the historically black cemetery that had fallen into disrepair. As Stacy observed when she went to investigate, all that remains of Columbian Harmony Cemetery is a nondescript plaque above the newsstands at the Rhode Island-Brentwood Metro Station, noting that, "Many distinguished black citizens including civil war veterans were buried in this cemetery. These bodies now rest in the New National Harmony Memorial Park Cemetery in Maryland." It's doubtful that many of the thousands of commuters who rush through the station each day have ever noticed.

This third cemetery is 7.3 miles from the Capitol. Stacy was able to speak with its historian, Mr. Sluby, who told her that letters were sent to family members of those interred at the older cemetery when the graves were initially moved from D.C. If they responded, new markers were installed, but if not, the bodies were simply reburied without identification. He explained that there were several notable African Americans with statues or markers dedicated to them at the new cemetery.

Philip Reed Remembered

Sadly, Philip Reed's exact final resting place will never be known, and it seems particularly unjust that he was repeatedly moved farther away from the statue of Freedom. Though a little more of his story is now known, an initiative to place a monument at Harmony Memorial Park Cemetery would be a small, but welcome addition to our nation's history to recognize this man who made such a significant and indelible contribution that every one of us can see when we visit America's Capitol. Was he there on December 2, 1863, when Freedom was put in place on top of the dome? I can't imagine that he wasn't.

CHAPTER SIXTEEN

No, Your Name Wasn't Changed at Ellis Island

Why you shouldn't fall for this popular myth

I BLAME IT on *The Godfather.* Well, that and immigrant grandfathers who enjoyed spinning yarns to confuse their offspring. In spite of what you've been told or what you still read in normally reliable sources, names were not changed at Ellis Island. All those stories you've heard about the last syllable of your surname being lopped off by some official who found it too cumbersome to pronounce? Not true. Young Sicilian immigrant Vito Andolini winding up with his hometown of Corleone as his surname due to a careless Ellis Island employee as seen in *The Godfather?* Wouldn't happen.

That's not to say that mistakes didn't occur, but they were rare because those who worked at Ellis Island—many foreign-born themselves and collectively speaking dozens of languages in order to communicate with fresh arrivals in their native tongues—verified passenger lists that were created in the country of departure. And even if great-granddad's name was

incorrectly recorded, there was no reason to stick with that distorted version once he passed through.

The truth is that many of our immigrant ancestors' names
were changed—*by them*—and after their brief interlude at Ellis
Island. But try telling that to anyone who can't find their ancestors in immigration databases. Our name must have been
changed there, they protest. Otherwise, we'd be able to find them
listed, but they're not there! I sympathize with this frustration
because it's true that many of our forebears are seemingly absent. But more often than not, they really are present and it's
possible to pry them out of their hiding places if you know what
to look for. With that in mind, I thought I'd share some of my
more memorable immigrant finds with the hope that these ex-
amples will give you ideas to improve the odds of excavating that
stubborn ancestor of yours.

An Opportunity to Practice Flexibility

In today's bureaucratic world, a misspelling of your name by
even a single letter can result in scrutiny in the security line at
the airport, second-guessing at the DMV, or the rejection of a
loan application, but that level of accuracy is a recent development. Most people alive in America today have grown up with
Social Security and all that entails, but until this system was
launched in 1936 and gradually became entrenched, we were
much more flexible about our names. My husband's uncles, for
instance—all American-born and raised in the same house in
the 1920s and '30s—spelled their last name differently. Some
went by Smolenyak and some by Smolenak, dropping the *y*. We
have no clue why this happened within the same nuclear family,
but it did and it wasn't all that unusual.

So if you happen to pride yourself on your spelling talents, my
advice is to get sloppy. As a Catholic school alumna who still has
the plastic Mother Mary statue I received for being the best girl

speller in the second grade, I can relate if this counsel pains you, but many people miss their ancestors in relevant databases because they're being too literal—often limiting themselves to the "correct" spelling. Think about it. Until 1917, there were no literacy requirements for those entering the country, so it's quite possible that Granddad arrived not knowing how to spell his own name. Or maybe he was literate, but from Russia, which uses the Cyrillic alphabet. Not all the letters transliterate exactly, which explains why a Smolenyak might be recorded as Smolenak, Szmolenak, and Smolenjak. To give you an idea of just how pronounced this untamed spelling can be, the twenty-one Smolenyaks who came to America are recorded fifteen different ways.

Then there's the matter of handwriting. The library at Ellis Island is named after beloved comedian Bob Hope, but even he resisted discovery when officials sought to honor him at an annual Ellis Island awards event about a decade ago. Born Leslie Townes Hope, he appears in the database as Leslie Hape when he immigrated in 1908. That single letter difference initially prevented researchers from identifying the first time he set foot on American soil, but that's just the beginning. Other sources give his name as Lester rather than Leslie, and of course, he eventually decided that he preferred to be called Bob. As an entertainer, he was a well-travelled man so it's possible to find later entries for him as:

- Leslie Hope
- Lester Hope
- Lester Bob Hope
- Lester T. Hope
- Lester Townes Hope

Bob Hope seems like such a simple name, but it offers plenty of room for distortion or interpretation. Now imagine what could happen with a name like Giuseppina Bernicchi Francesconi.

There's also the issue of nicknames and American versions of names that were unfamiliar here. For instance, rocker and *Celebrity Apprentice* winner Bret Michaels was born Bret Michael Sychak—a name that starts and ends like my own—so I decided to see whether he might share my Carpatho-Rusyn heritage. Eventually, I confirmed that he did, but his great-grandfather, Vasil Sychak, didn't give up his origins easily. Most immigrant Vasils altered their names to Basil or William, but Bret's ancestor opted for Wallace, though he had a habit of spelling it Valles. Sychak offers its own complications, so I had to try countless creative combinations of possible first and last names to find his arrival. Odds are that only the most thorough and patient of his descendants would have ever found his record if they went looking for it. Over time, I've become familiar with these old-to-new transitions—Jurko to George, Jean to John, Wojtek to Albert (I've never really understood this one, but it's quite common), Mathias to Matthew—but a quick cheat that's always worth a try is simply searching without any first name.

Originating documents can also be the source of errors. In the case of Annie Moore, the first Ellis Island immigrant, she and her brothers are accurately recorded as Annie, Anthony, and Phillip upon arrival, but in their departure records from Queenstown (now Cork), they're listed as Annie, Anthon, and Fillik. Whoever noted their names here not only didn't change them as is so often claimed, but actually corrected mistakes made on the other side of the ocean. Those who feel the need to point an accusatory finger might need to take a closer look at the ports of Bremen, Antwerp, and Naples.

It's even possible that Grandma didn't come through Ellis Island at all in spite of the fact that she always claimed she did. I can't tell you how many times people have insisted that their ancestor arrived at Ellis Island, only to ultimately learn that they came before it even existed or entered through one of more than a hundred other ports. Ellis Island has become almost synonymous with immigration in America, so there's a tendency to connect the two regardless of the specifics of an individual's arrival. So if you can't find Grandma in New York, don't be surprised to spy her in Boston, New Orleans, Philadelphia, Galveston, or crossing the Mexican border.

More Immigrant Quirks

Let's say you've managed to outwit the bizarre spellings and Johnification of the Jean, Johannes, or Giovanni in your family tree, but there's still an ancestor who's refusing to come out of hiding. What else can you try?

If you're dealing with an Italian immigrant, think in terms of maiden names. A typical pattern was for the father to come first, make a little money, and then send back for his wife and kids. It's the wife and kids who can often be elusive because Italian women retained their maiden names after marriage and so frequently traveled that way. And the kids? Sometimes they used Mom's surname since they were with her and sometimes they used Dad's. This is exactly what I ran into with my husband's family—and with Al Capone's. Al Capone's mother and big brothers came to join his father in Brooklyn in 1895. As it happens, his brothers Raffaele and Vincenzo are listed as Capones, but their mother—on the line above them—is recorded as Teresa Raiola. Had I fixated on Teresa Capone, I'd still be looking for her. Before long, Raffaele became Ralph and Vincenzo eventually changed his name to Richard Hart—a radical modification that made it difficult for his own family to find him for many years.

Another ethnic peculiarity is the Scandinavian use of both farm and patronymic names—that is, surnames derived from location and Dad's name. Patronymics are why so many of Scandinavian ancestry have names that end in –son: Johnson, Peterson, Anderson, and so forth. Like Bob Hope, football great Knute Rockne was honored at the annual Ellis Island awards that pay tribute to immigrants and their descendants. And like Bob Hope, he was skulking in the depths of the database. I eventually found him as Knud Larsen (note the spelling variation between Knute and Knud), and he was indeed, the son of man named Lars. In fact, his full name was given as Knud Larsen Rohne (*k*'s and *h*'s are often confused with each other), but this slight variation of Rokne was only recorded with ditto marks under his mother's surname and the transcriber had failed to spot the marks. The absence of the somewhat distinctive Rokne surname plunged the future coach into a sea of ninety-five other Knud Larsens, rendering him next to invisible. How did I find him? Through his mother. When I couldn't find Knute, I went looking for his mother, Martha Pedersen Rokne, and eventually turned up the family's 1893 arrival—a back-dooring approach I often use when stuck.

And when it comes to immigration, it's men who lie about their ages, rather than women. Why? Because they were avoiding the draft. Many ethnicities seem to think that it's unique to them, but quite a few European governments mandated military service for men of a certain age, often extending to minorities who had no loyalty to the government in question. For that reason, it was quite common to shuffle males in the family out of the country when they were approaching draft age. But due to fears that they would be stopped at the border, they were sometimes equipped with papers that under- or overstated their ages. On some occasions, they might even travel under another man's documents. Such was the case with my own immigrant great-grandfather who morphed from a Peter to an Andras and experienced a ten-year age swing during the course of his two-week journey from Hamburg to New York. Yet another reason to be flexible when digging through databases.

After Ellis

Up until now, I've mostly been sharing ways our ancestors can be unintentionally concealed in databases, but as I mentioned at the outset, many names were deliberately changed by the immigrant himself after his encounter with Ellis Island. And more often than not, it's these after-the-fact alterations that wind up making our ancestors invisible. This is because the insistence on believing that the name change was foisted upon them at Ellis Island causes their descendants to search for them under their Americanized name. If a culturally myopic official decided on the spot to shorten Grandpa's name while registering him, then he should be listed under this new name, right? Not so much.

Case in point. A few years ago, I read an article about Los Angeles landmark Pink's Hot Dogs. Easily the most famous hot dog stand in the world, it's as popular now as it was when founded in 1939 by Paul Pink. Paul Pink was born in 1908 to immigrant parents in Minnesota, so I suppose I shouldn't have been surprised when this article about the 70th anniversary of the iconic eatery included the following classic chestnut: "When Romanian immigrant Isadore Pinkowitz landed on Ellis Island in the early 1900s, immigration officials shortened and Americanized his name to Pink." I sighed when I read this and took about twenty minutes to find the truth. The Ellis Island record for Paul Pink's parents is shown below.

I did this by backtracking through the lives of Paul and his

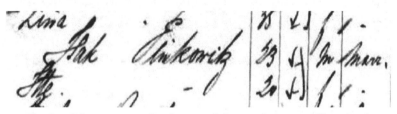

The family's name was clearly recorded as Pinkowitz at Ellis Island.
(National Archives and Records Administration)

parents using census and military records, supplemented with birth and death indexes. This is definitely the arrival of his parents on July 1, 1900, and Paul's mother, Etta, was evidently pregnant during the journey because just eight and a half months later, she gave birth to their first child in America—a child who was given the surname of Pink. The reason we chow down on Pink's hot dogs today instead of Pinkowitz's is Isadore's decision to lop two syllables off of his name, not that of an Ellis Island clerk who couldn't be bothered with five more letters.

And while the trim-a-few-letters approach is a popular one, another tactic used by ancestors seeking to assimilate as quickly as possible is direct translation. I recall an army case of mine when I was convinced that I had spotted the soldier's sisters in the California death index. All the other details fit, but their maiden name was given as Fox instead of the Czech surname I was expecting. Using Google Translate, it took just moments to determine that my hunch was correct; they had changed the family name from *Liška*, the Czech word for "fox," to its English equivalent. They were indeed the soldier's sisters.

Nor are these changes limited to the first post-immigration years or even the immigrant generation. In my own family, one branch defied my efforts to track them down even though I knew which state they had moved to back in the 1930s. Finally, one of them found me. That's how I learned that a journalist in the family had decided that Smolenyak was too complicated a name for her profession, so decided to pick a new name that shared a couple of letters in common with the original: Simmons. This was the 1960s, some three-quarters of a century after our immigrant ancestor arrived. More curious still is the fact that her parents opted to follow her lead and switched to Simmons as well. But this isn't the most surprising, delayed name change I've encountered in my research. That honor is reserved for a third-generation American who adopted the surname of Murgatroyd. His original name? Sinatra.

Mind Games

Over the years, I've enjoyed tussling with our immigrant ancestors to force them from their hiding places, but my favorite case so far involved one of Steven Tyler's grandfathers. When Tyler was selected to be an *American Idol* judge, I decided to take a peek into his past for a column I write. Tyler is an Americanization of Tallarico, the Italian name that was passed down by his paternal grandfather, but it was his maternal, Polish/Russian grandfather, Felix Blancha, who caught my eye. Being half-Slavic myself, I know what it's like to deal with the constantly changing borders of Eastern Europe. Many people of our heritage grew up hearing an old joke about Grandpa living in four countries, but never moving from the house he was born in—all thanks to the borders shifting around him. And that's what leads to the confusion over Felix's origin.

It took some effort, but I finally found his arrival on the *President Lincoln* in 1914. His journey was well timed; had it been any later, WWI probably would have prevented his immigration. Still, it must have been a rough trip for him since he was detained in the hospital at Ellis Island before eventually being released. On the ship's manifest, Felix claimed Bobruysk as his hometown. Bobruysk is now in Belarus, but his paper trail clearly indicates that he regarded himself as Polish—that, and his name.

You might think that Blancha doesn't sound particularly Polish, and I'd have to agree. In fact, once I found it, I immediately thought that he must have Americanized it, so I went looking for fellows named Felix with surnames that looked like *bialy*, the Polish word for white. With the similar letters and meaning, I figured he must have dreamed up the Blancha version, but the joke was on me.

I like a good challenge, and get bored when our ancestors are too easy to trace, but even so, I didn't anticipate the mind game that Tyler's grandfather played. I tried all the usual tricks for finding his original last name, but none of them panned out. Naturalization and court records kept his secret safe, but then I found his marriage record, and couldn't help but laugh. His real name was Czarnyszewicz.

I've delved into enough Slavic-language records to realize what he had done. Czarny is Polish for black. Felix had changed his name from Czarnyszewicz to Blancha—from black to white. He made this colorful flip roughly a decade after coming to America, but what do you want to bet that his descendants think his name was changed at Ellis Island?

CHAPTER SEVENTEEN

Paralyzed Prostitute

Following the trail of an Oregon madam

YES, I KNOW these two words don't usually go together, but they actually describe the subject of this particular roots quest. I get pulled into research projects many different ways. This one was triggered by one of those "Hey, Megan, this sounds like you" shout-outs. Within the genealogical community, I'm known for having a hard time resisting a history mystery, so whenever a journalist writes about a military medal someone wants to return to a descendant of the soldier, a tombstone that showed up where it didn't belong, a puzzle that could be tackled through DNA, or some other historical riddle, I will inevitably get a few e-mails, Facebook postings, and tweets.

In this case, a friend on the West Coast called me about an article that appeared in the *Baker City Herald*. Entitled "The Mystery of Mabel," it told of the struggles of Betty Wontorek of Orange, California, to find out what had become of her maternal grandmother, Mabel Cavin.

Normally, when we think of Victorian-era ancestors, we think

of conservative, stern-looking folks trapped in sepia-toned photos, but according to the article, Mabel didn't fit this mold, probably due to an event that occurred in her youth:

> She was crippled at age seven—her left side almost com-
> pletely paralyzed—when she fell on a fence post and be-
> came a life-long addict to morphine, or that era's
> painkiller, a non-prescription opiate called laudanum.

Wontorek speculated that it was this incident, which would
have limited her means of making a living, that led Mabel to
eventually become a prostitute, apparently known in Baker City
as Madam Jeanetta.

Betty's matter-of-fact attitude about her grandmother appealed to me. I liked that she was not only ready to claim this colorful ancestor, but actively seeking to learn more about her. But
her task was made more difficult because her mother, one of a
number of children Mabel apparently had and put up for adoption, was killed in an accident back in 1963. To compound her
woes, Betty's father had been killed in World War II, so she
couldn't turn to him for information about her mother's family.
On the upside, her mother had started investigating her past before her untimely death and managed to learn that she had been
born Beatrice Eva Whitworth to Mabel and Andrew Whitworth
in Baker City, Oregon. She had also succeeded in finding one of
her birth siblings, but this sister had died in 1980, so she was no
longer a possible resource for Betty. It was by talking to Baker
City old-timers still alive back in the 1950s that Betty's mother
had learned about Mabel's unconventional history, yet no one
could recall what had become of her. Betty was determined to
find out, but encountered challenges she suspected were due to
embarrassment caused by Mabel's choice of profession. Still, she
felt compassion for her lost soul of a grandmother and refused to
accept her absence from the family tree.

People tend to have one of two reactions to the discovery of black sheep ancestors: we hide them or we celebrate them. And when we hide them, a wall of silence descends, making it difficult for ensuing generations to learn the truth. This is exactly what Betty was dealing with. In spite of this feature article detailing her hunt in the Baker City newspaper—a smart strategy on Betty's part—she was still no closer to solving the mystery of Mabel, so when it came to my attention, I decided to help. Little did I know, though, just how complicated Mabel's life had been.

Making Sense of the Census

"Making sense of the census" is a favorite pun of hardcore genealogists, but aptly describes the heart of this case. The U.S. census, conducted by the federal government in all the years ending with "0" since 1790, is the most heavily used document collection by American researchers. Loaded with names, dates, places, and relationships—the building blocks of genealogy—it provides snapshots of families over time, so is frequently the first resource consulted. It was a no-brainer that this was where I would begin.

Equipped with all the information Betty had already gathered, it took just moments to find Mabel in the 1900 census. There she was with her parents, Ambros and Julia Cavin, a brother, an uncle, and a boarder. All the details mapped with what Betty had shared. So far, so good.

Then I slammed into a brick wall. There was no sign of a Mabel Cavin or Whitworth in the 1910, 1920, or 1930 census. Sure, there were women named Mabel of a likely age in each of them, but how could I tell if any was her? Though census takers could sometimes be remarkably blunt, recording occupations such as prostitute, concubine, whore, harlot, pleasure girl, trick woman, and soiled dove, none of these was attached to any of the Mabels I found in the vicinity.

Of course, that was assuming she had stayed put. Now I

understood why Betty was having such a hard time picking up her grandmother's trail.

Going Local

After flailing around for a bit trying to find any trace of Mabel, I decided I needed some help on the ground in Oregon, so I hired a researcher named Pat Wahl in Salem, Oregon, home to the state archives. I had been there once myself researching an Irish branch of my family that had gone west, so I knew what an outstanding repository it was, and I wasn't disappointed. Before long, Pat sent me a state census that had been conducted in 1905. Just as with the 1900 census Mabel was living with her parents and brother, so where had she vanished to between 1905 and 1910?

One of the best reasons to work with local genealogists is that they have knowledge of and access to wonderful resources that might otherwise go overlooked. Imagine my reaction when Pat included a couple of articles about Mabel's mother, Julia— one from 1911 about her arrest for running a "disorderly house," and another from 1909 telling of a twenty-six-year-old prostitute dying of alcoholism in Julia's lodging house.

Until then, I had been under the impression that Mabel had somehow gone astray. The two census records she appeared in seemed to place her in the midst of a normal, nuclear family. There had been no hints of her mother's involvement in the "world's oldest profession," but now I shifted to a new paradigm.

Noticing that the two articles were from 1909 and 1911, I realized that Mabel's mother must have been in Baker City at the time of the 1910 census. Taking a second look, I found Julia, but listed as Frances. Mabel's brother was there as well, but had changed names from William Walter to Richard. No wonder they had escaped my attention earlier. I wasn't sure why all this experimentation with names was going on, but thought they might have considered it prudent given what seemed to be emerging as the family business. Julia/Frances was recorded as the widowed proprietor of a rooming house, which I now recognized as a euphemism for madam. I wondered whether perhaps Mabel's involvement in the trade was a warped form of nepotism, but there was still no sign of her. There was, however, a clue.

In the same residence was a five-year-old boy named Richard Sills who was noted as the grandson of Julia/Frances. Since Mabel only had one brother, this had to have been her son, given that any child of her brother's would have been named Cavin. This, then, was one of the other children she had put up for adoption, although it seemed more accurate to say that she had left him with her mother.

On the Husband Trail

At this point, things started to get complicated. To help you follow along, I'll run a tally as I share my discoveries of Mabel's assorted husbands and children. Clearly she must have married a man named Sills, probably husband number one. Thinking this marriage would have most likely occurred in Baker City, I decided to hire another local researcher, but this time, one who lived near Mabel's former stomping grounds. Kathleen Christensen swiftly dug in and found her 1904 marriage to William L. Sills. The marriage must have been a short one since she was living with her parents in the 1905 census, presumably taken before the birth of her son that year. *Tally: One husband and one child.*

The absence of a Mabel Sills in the 1910 census suggested that she might have married again. Sure enough, a search of Baker City marriage records turned up a Mabel Sills marrying J. A. Leishman in June 1909. Curiously, her father, Ambros, was a witness to the ceremony, something of a surprise since her mother was supposedly widowed by the following year. While it was certainly possible that he had died in this narrow time frame, I was starting to get a feel for the family by now and suspected I might be dealing with another fiction, so I asked Kathleen to search for divorce records. In 1910, Julia had sued for divorce and lost, but in 1913, Ambros had returned the favor and prevailed. Ambros, I would later learn, moved to Idaho, remarried and lived until 1932.

Armed with her new married name, I returned to the 1910 census looking for Mabel with husband number two, and finally found her as "Mable" Leish. Why the marriage record had added a–*man* to the end of Leish, I don't know, but such a red herring seemed trivial by now. She was living in the home of her parents-in-law with her husband, Julius, and their five-month-old son, William, but not for long. *Tally: Two husbands and two children.*

Divorce records for the county showed that Mabel charged Julius with neglect of both her and their son, William. Julius countersued claiming that she was the one guilty of neglect. On November 5, 1913, the divorce was granted, but rather extraordinarily for the times, Julius received sole custody of their child. This ruling definitely stuck because the 1920 census found Julius remarried, but still retaining custody of William. What the divorce decree failed to mention is that there had been another child, a daughter, seemingly the first to have been put up for adoption. *Tally: Two husbands and three children.*

The husbands and children were starting to stack up. William L. Sills in 1904 and Julius A. Leish in 1909 (and at least two sons and a daughter along the way), and from what Betty had told me from the outset, I knew there was an Andrew Whitworth somewhere in the mix. I didn't have far to look because a week to the day after her divorce to Leish was finalized, Mabel married Andy Whitworth. *Tally: Three husbands and three children.*

They say that past performance is not necessarily indicative of future results, but in Mabel's case, it was. Betty knew that her mother had been born to Andy and Mabel Whitworth in 1917, but their divorce papers of 1918 made no mention of her. They did, however, mention another daughter, Geneva. Just like the last marriage—brief with two children, one kept and one put up for adoption. *Tally: Three husbands and five children.*

This time Mabel waited six whole weeks from September 16th, the date of her divorce, before remarrying on October 31st to Arthur B. Davis. And true to form, in the 1920 census, her daughter Geneva Whitworth was living with her ex-husband. In fact, though there's no trace of Mabel in the 1920 census, three of her children from three different marriages were scattered around Baker City—two with their fathers and one with an aunt and uncle. *Tally: Four husbands and five children.*

This 1918 marriage would prove to be Mabel's last, and perhaps by then, she was getting sheepish about it because she was recorded not as Mabel, but as Jeannette P. Whitworth. The article that had prompted this whole undertaking stated that Mabel was a lady of the evening who went by "Madam Jeanetta," but Madam had one more surprise for me. In the 1930 census, I found her as Jeannette Davis. Her occupation? Card reading.

Who's the Madam?

At this point, I was dizzy from trying to follow in Mabel's wake. Though I've given the abbreviated version here, Kathleen and I had been ping-ponging through countless rounds of requests and results to get this far. And now I was left wondering whether the madam part of Mabel's nickname derived from her later profession as a psychic or was perhaps a natural extension from her aging out of her first career. After all, her mother had been a madam.

Still, I had come a long way in answering Betty's question about what had become of her grandmother. Now all I had to figure out was where and when she had passed away and where she was buried. Turning back to Pat Wahl at the state archives, I asked for the death certificates of Mabel and her mother. It hadn't been possible to do this until I managed to unearth Mabel's final married surname.

The death certificate of Mabel's mother, Julia, tossed one more revelation my way. She had died in 1916 from edema of the lungs resulting from twenty years of "morphinism." In other words, she had been addicted to morphine. And from the newspaper articles found earlier, I knew that she had been a madam. I considered the possibility that the details of Julia's life had been transposed to that of her daughter. True, Mabel had made some poor decisions. She had run through a string of four marriages in fourteen years and had at least five children in that time, all of whom she had abandoned in one way or another. She was no saint, but even if she had been a prostitute, it seemed she had come by it naturally.

Mabel had died in 1936. Both she and her mother were buried in Mount Hope Cemetery, so I had a final request for Kathleen: find obituaries for mother and daughter and take photos of their tombstones. Although Julia had to endure the occasional arrest, the importance of a madam in a western mining town a century ago could be seen from the fact that she had both a front-page obituary lamenting her loss and a prominent tombstone. And Mabel? A fleeting mention buried in back pages and a patch of grass. Clearly, madams mattered.

I shared my wild ride with Betty. Mabel's story underscored that the truth is often so much more complicated than the digest version that's handed down to us, but all that Betty cared about was that she finally knew what had become of her grandmother. Thanking me in her inimitable Betty style, she paid me the highest compliment you can give to a name-conscious genealogist. "I'm so thankful," she exclaimed, "that if I were in my child-bearing years, I would name a girl Megan!"

CHAPTER EIGHTEEN

Half a Negro Boy

Finding a hidden connection between
Al Sharpton and Strom Thurmond

IT'S OFTEN BEEN SAID that politics makes strange bedfellows, and based on my experience, the same is true of genealogy. Few of us truly grasp how interconnected we all are, so I especially enjoy unearthing links that no one would have ever expected. That's exactly what happened when I discovered that Al Sharpton's great-grandfather, Coleman, had been owned by relatives of Strom Thurmond.

Mind you, I didn't see this coming. Nor did Rev. Al, who didn't even know that he had roots in South Carolina, much less any tie to the Thurmond family. In 1948, Strom Thurmond ran for president on a platform of racial segregation, and in 2004, civil rights activist Sharpton ran for the same office on a platform of racial justice. Descendants of slave owners and slaves, respectively, both championed what would have undoubtedly been their ancestors' perspectives and causes. That the latter is the progeny of slaves owned by ancestors of the former says something about

the recent history of America, but it also reminds us that our
roots often claim us in ways we don't realize.

Why Rev. Al's Roots?

How was it that I came to research Al Sharpton's roots in the
first place? Truth be told, it was almost an accident. It was January 2007 and I had recently come on board with Ancestry.com
as the company's chief family historian. February was approaching and Ancestry decided to announce the launch of its
African American Historical Records Collection during Black
History Month. In an effort to secure coverage for the launch,
Ancestry reached out to a number of journalists. Austin Fenner,
then with the *New York Daily News,* initially took a pass, but said
he might reconsider if we would agree to research a celebrity's
roots for the article. He intended this as a test to see just how useful the new record collection was, and Ancestry readily agreed,
leaving the choice of celebrity to Fenner.

Fenner had recently traveled to South Carolina for the funeral
of the Godfather of Soul, James Brown. When Brown's son was
killed in a car accident back in the 1970s, Sharpton became something of a substitute son and the two were extremely close. Sharpton, who credits Brown with teaching him "to be a man," was
heartbroken at Brown's loss and officiated at his funeral. It was
probably this recent encounter that led Fenner to select Sharpton,
though neither of them had any reason to suspect that it would
soon cause them both to U-turn to South Carolina. It didn't take
long to get Sharpton's approval, and then the search was on.

What Can You Find Out in Forty-eight Hours?

As is often the case with celebrity research, I had to start digging before receiving any input from Sharpton's "people." Fenner

had challenged Ancestry, asking what could be found in a mere forty-eight hours, so I had no time to waste. I suppose I should confess that I have mixed feelings about such requests. The hard-core genealogist in me feels obligated to point out that genealogy isn't the instant pudding that many now perceive it to be, but another part loves setting the bar high and putting my sleuthing to the test. I had no choice in this particular matter, so subdued the it's-not-that-easy thoughts orbiting my brain, and dove into the case with around-the-clock vigor. As I expected would happen, by the time I received the basic information I requested (names and a few details about Sharpton's parents and grandparents), it simply served as confirmation of what I had already figured out.

Before I knew it, I was in a small conference room in Manhattan with Fenner to present my findings. With us were several PR folks and Tony Burroughs, a well-known expert in African American genealogy whom we thought might be able to provide additional insight as we waded through Sharpton's family tree. Sharpton himself wasn't with us, but the assumption was that we'd share everything with him when his schedule permitted.

Fenner was perhaps the most methodical journalist I've ever worked with. I appreciated that he took his time making sure to get every detail right, so we soldiered through name after name, branch after branch, document after document. To get to this point, I first identified Sharpton's parents and grandparents. Because my research has since been shared publicly, you can now google your way to this information, but at the time, it took some doing to find out their names. While you might think these recent generations would be the easiest to research, they're often the most difficult due to privacy laws that protect the living. Consequently, I often wind up stitching together these initial relationships by interweaving tidbits found in a variety of newspaper, court, and property records, which is what I did in this case. From there, I used conventional online research in conjunction with much pleading with a number of on-the-ground researchers in the South and Salt Lake City to let me jump ahead of other customers they had in line. When I make requests of local researchers, I explain exactly what I'm looking for, often to the level of specifying which roll of microfilm they'll find a particular document on. Using these tactics, I climbed several generations back through each of the branches of his family tree in preparation for the meeting.

An Uncomfortable Moment

Perhaps an hour into the interview, we arrived at Coleman Sharpton, one of Al Sharpton's great-grandfathers. When first venturing into genealogy, most of us begin by focusing on the surname we were born with, so I assumed that this branch would be of particular interest. Al Sharpton was born in New York to Florida and Alabama-born parents, but didn't know much more than that. I had gone back to his grandfather, Coleman Jr., and *his* father, Coleman Sr. It was apparent to me that Coleman Sr. had once been a slave, and I said as much to Fenner. I also stated that the odds were good that he had been owned by a Sharpton family.

At this juncture, Burroughs objected. He said that I could make no such claim, that I had no proof. This was an awkward moment. Technically, he was right. I didn't have a document that proved beyond a shadow of a doubt that Coleman Sharpton had been a slave, but all the signs were there. Though born in South Carolina, he was living in Liberty County, Florida, slightly post-Emancipation, and there had been a white, slave-owning family of the same surname in the same location in the 1860 census. In fact, these were the only Sharptons living in all of Florida in 1860, and not so incidentally, the elder members of this family had also been born in South Carolina. Other indicators (for instance, Coleman's non-appearance in any pre-Emancipation census records) supported my assertion, so it didn't take much to connect the dots.

I didn't mind that Burroughs had raised this objection, but was taken aback that he did so in front of a journalist instead of earlier. We both knew that my claims were well justified, so at the time, it felt almost as if I were doing an interview with a sniper in the room. I was running on fumes, having had little sleep, due to the forty-eight hour time limit and hadn't expected Tony (I've been referring to him as Burroughs, but in everyday life, he's my friend Tony) to take a shot at my research, but as things would evolve, he had done us all a favor. Acknowledging his qualification, I then explained that Coleman Sharpton was probably originally from Edgefield County, South Carolina, as that was where the white Sharpton family once lived. At this point, Tony offered an observation that would prove helpful, though I didn't realize it at the time. He explained that some of his own ancestry traced to Edgefield County and described it as "Thurmond territory" with a violent past.

We moved on to the rest of Sharpton's heritage, and concluded the interview. Fenner was impressed—so impressed that he gave me more time to do additional research. He wanted to know what else I might be able to find out with a little more breathing room. Not surprisingly, one of the first items on my new to-do list was to sniff out any documents that would substantiate my statements about Coleman.

The Thurmond Connection

The next time we all met—again without Sharpton—I was better equipped. Much had transpired, especially regarding Coleman. It had taken extensive digging at several repositories in both Florida and South Carolina court records. Liberty County in Florida had proven particularly difficult as it had been carved out of Gadsden County in 1855, the period of greatest interest, and records for the two counties had become both intermingled and dispersed. Finding relevant records turned into something of a scavenger hunt, but with a bit of effort, I was able to get help from talented, local researchers like Jack Butler. As with the first round of research, much begging and nudging was involved because the clock was still ticking, albeit less loudly.

When it comes to picking up the trail of those who have been enslaved, there are no guarantees. I didn't know whether Coleman would have left a trace in the property records of his owner, but I was optimistic that if he had, I would be able to spot him due to his distinctive first name. What I would eventually learn is that Coleman had left a remarkable paper trail.

Yes, he had been owned by the white Sharpton family of Liberty County, Florida, as I had suspected, but there was more to the story than that. His last owners were a four-pack of Sharpton children who inherited Coleman when their father died broke and without a will. Their grandfather back in South Carolina decided to help out his widowed daughter-in-law and grandchildren by sending several slaves to Florida to be leased out to help pay off his deceased son's debts. Coleman was one of these slaves.

Curious about the children who had last owned Coleman, I researched them and swiftly identified their mother as Julia Ann Thurmond. As soon as I saw the name, I flashed back to the earlier meeting when Tony Burroughs had referred to Edgefield County as "Thurmond territory." Could there be a connection to Strom Thurmond?

I didn't jump to conclusions because Thurmond was a common name in the region, but I shifted into find-a-link mode, experimenting with different possibilities. I think of it as akin to playing with a Rubik's cube, twisting and turning this way and that to see if it would all fall into place. Several hours later, I figured out that the pieces did indeed fit. Julia was Strom's first cousin twice removed, so Coleman's last owners were relatives of Strom Thurmond. I'm not sure why, but these breakthroughs always seem to come when I'm sitting at my desk at an obscene hour when it would be inappropriate for me to call anyone to share the news, so I just sat there and took it in—a hidden connection, ironically tucked away in a county named Liberty, between two presidential candidates who had campaigned on such diametrically opposed platforms.

The Reveal

Whatever the nature of the revelation, I love the moment when I first smoke out something that's been previously unknown. As on other occasions before and since, I was jazzed. But in this case, the rush of discovery was seriously tempered. What, I wondered, would Sharpton think?

It had taken all of four days to find the document that linked Al Sharpton's and Strom Thurmond's families, but I have to stress how exceptional this is. Many doing African American research may never find such a record, and even if found, the time involved would usually be measured in months or years, rather than days. It was part skill and part luck that I had uncovered so much so fast, and now that I had a fuller understanding of Coleman's life, it was time to meet with Fenner again.

The same group reconvened in the same conference room, and Fenner got far more than he had bargained for. What had begun as a human-interest story was morphing into front-page news. I walked all present through the latest developments. Now there was solid proof of the claims I had made the last time.

All that was left to do was to share the outcome of the research with Reverend Sharpton. Fenner arranged a meeting that Sharpton probably attended only out of a sense of obligation since he had agreed to the research. As he later explained, he perceived all this as "at best, some Black History Month paragraph."

Yet again, we all gathered, but this time in Sharpton's New York City radio studio (the same one where he and Imus would meet a couple of months later to discuss racist remarks made about the Rutgers University women's basketball team). Not wanting to rush it, I went branch by branch through his ancestry.

He probably wondered why I left his Sharpton branch for last, but when we arrived there, his interest perked up considerably as I followed it back from Florida to South Carolina. He had known so little about this part of his family that even the connection to South Carolina was news to him, and as I would later learn, he was entertaining hope that I might be steering him toward a hitherto unknown relationship with his recently departed friend and mentor, James Brown.

It's funny what your memory chooses to freeze-frame, and what stands out in my mind is that Sharpton was eating hot and sour soup when I spelled everything out for him. A busy man, he has to multitask, and photos show that I was more or less kneeling beside him to show him various documents as he sipped his soup. Thanks to Fenner's detailed recording of the meeting in a *Daily News* article, I also know exactly what we both said when I broached the delicate matter of the Thurmond connection, an exchange that was brief but tense as Sharpton digested my meaning:

> SMOLENYAK: "Their mother was a Thurmond. Julia Ann Thurmond."
> SHARPTON: "Was what?"
> SMOLENYAK: "A Thurmond. Jefferson Sharpton's wife was a Thurmond. These children, who were the last owners of Coleman, were related to Strom Thurmond through their mother."
> SHARPTON: "Strom Thurmond's family owned my family."

It's Sharpton's silence that I remember best. Rev. Al is never at a loss for words, so it almost scared me, though it wasn't entirely unexpected. Having walked others through details pertaining to their once-enslaved ancestors, I've come to believe that it's one thing to know on an intellectual level that your ancestors were slaves, but another entirely to know the specifics. To know that your great-grandfather, Coleman Sharpton, was a slave, where

Author explaining unexpected discovery to Al Sharpton. (Author)

he was born, where he lived, and who owned him takes slavery from the abstract to a fierce reality. To look at documents that prove it all makes it impossible to escape. And that takes time to absorb. That's what Sharpton was doing in his silence.

Heading South

After this, everything is almost a blur to me. Austin Fenner wrote an article that appeared perhaps a week later on the front page of the *Daily News.* I was scheduled to appear at a news conference that day with Sharpton in New York City, but was snowed in from another event in Chicago, so I didn't make it, but the story lingered. Sharpton had agreed to have his roots explored, and as a result, now had an unexpected travel companion: me.

I recall feeling almost like a stalker as I followed in his wake. I began by speaking at his church in Harlem (no pressure there, speaking in between orators Al Sharpton and Jesse Jackson!), and before it was over, I would trail him to Alabama, Georgia, Tennessee, and South Carolina. He and I would do countless radio interviews and live remotes, and recount the revelation and his response over and over. He told each audience how he had hung the slave records in his house to remind him that, "We have an obligation to those who never had the options we do, but held on so that we could exist." The revelation, he said, had redoubled his commitment.

Of this meandering journey, it was Edgefield, South Carolina, that was most memorable. I had road-tripped from Selma, Alabama, the previous day and only arrived in town late the night before. This was distressing as I wanted to scope out the area before dealing with camera crews and interviews the next morning, but there was no time. The following morning, I found myself in the hotel lobby awaiting the people I was traveling with and unintentionally eavesdropping on a local educators group as they discussed Sharpton's imminent arrival in Edgefield. All but one were displeased, so it was a strange experience to be in their midst, hidden in plain sight.

I grew impatient as I waited for the others, and distracted myself by examining the old maps that adorned the lobby. Genealogists love maps, so I was almost giddy when I realized that they were maps from Edgefield in the 1800s. I hadn't had the chance to explore, but thanks to these maps, I was able to discern that the cemetery where the media, Sharpton's entourage, and I were all meeting was very close to the property that had once been owned by the Sharpton and Thurmond families. I had expected us all to meet at the county courthouse and wasn't sure why the location had been shifted to the cemetery, but welcomed this last-minute snippet of insight.

By the time we made our way to the cemetery, CNN, CBS, and others were already in place. I quickly scanned the graveyard and found only a single tombstone with a relevant name, and though those buried there had died long ago, it had been recently replaced by a caring descendant. While this spoke well of the family, I was less than thrilled as I knew that it would make for unexciting footage. Fortunately, I had invited two locals, Tonya Browder and Wayne O'Bryant, who had helped me with the research. Once I heard of the change of location, I had given them a quick call to redirect them to the cemetery. Now pondering what to discuss when Sharpton arrived, I queried them about the maps I had seen in the hotel lobby. That's when I learned that the house was still standing at the plantation where Coleman would have once lived. I immediately made an executive decision that we would all be convoying over to the plantation as soon as we had onced around the cemetery.

Sharpton arrived soon after. I greeted him and explained the tombstone, and then we all climbed back into our SUVs. The present property owner took the arrival of the media blitzkrieg in stride and guided Sharpton around the property. Something of a historical purist, he had left the manor house and grounds in close to original (though somewhat dilapidated) condition, so it was effectively a time capsule. Even more remarkably, a one-time slave cabin remained in the back. At one point, our guide reached down and scooped up a horseshoe. Handing it to Sharpton, he said, "Why don't you take this? One of your ancestors probably made it." A quick traipse through the woods to the small, unmarked stones of the slaves' cemetery completed the tour, and the swarm left as quickly as it had descended perhaps an hour earlier.

Coleman Wanted His Story Told

Though it must have felt odd to have a genealogist attached at the hip, Rev. Al tolerated my frequent presence well, but we rarely had time to talk about anything beyond the necessary.

There were, however, a few quiet moments during breaks in his radio shows (if memory serves, I was a guest on four of them), and that's when we managed to have brief chats.

It was during one of these lulls that I commented on the lack of attention being given to one of the most astonishing aspects of this story. I understood the fascination with the connection between Al Sharpton and Strom Thurmond, of course, but my research had surfaced several other documents that were almost completely ignored. Coleman, it turned out, had already been shuffled among various owners twice by the age of four, leaving a considerable paper trail. Coleman, I told Sharpton, was screaming to be heard.

When his first owner died, he was jointly inherited by a son and son-in-law of that man. Catching everyone off guard, the son-in-law died later that same year. I wondered where that might have left Coleman, so I ordered a copy of the son-in-law's estate papers. And that's where I found the notation that almost made me choke. The original owner's son had bought out his brother-in-law's share of Coleman from his estate. In other words, he had purchased "half of a Negro boy Coleman."

When I explained this to Sharpton, he responded that it was almost as if his ancestor had been a box of soap that could be bought off the shelf at the local department store. I could see the parallel, but the truth is that it was worse than that. You can't buy half a box of soap, but not too long ago, it was acceptable—normal, even—to buy half a human being. And that, to me, was as close as you can come to an instant education on slavery.

We heard you, Coleman.

Six words that speak volumes. (Edgefield County)

CHAPTER NINETEEN

A Lonely Tombstone on the Sidewalks of Manhattan

The wandering memorial of a Jewish pioneer goes home

TOMBSTONES WANDER. Teenagers get into mischief, developers upend inconvenient graveyards and scatter the holdings, and the occasional dimwit helps himself to "building materials" for his new patio. But sometimes they seemingly meander of their own accord, as if they had become restless in their final resting spot. Such was the case with Hinda Amchanitzky's tombstone.

No one knew how her memorial found its way to the concrete sidewalks of the Lower East Side in Manhattan, but that's where New Yorker John Lankenau found it leaning against a fire hydrant while walking his dog one evening. Many would have regarded the incongruous slab of granite as a curiosity and walked on. Others might have contemplated a rescue of sorts, but had second thoughts upon registering its weight of several hundred pounds. But not John. He took it home for safekeeping.

Aside from her name and "died May 15, 1910," all the writing on the stone was in Hebrew. Not Jewish himself, John reached out to several synagogues and Jewish genealogical societies, but no one was able to assist. Working the Internet, he found references to H. Amchanitzki, the author of a cookbook, but wasn't able to determine if the writer was Hinda. Over the next few years, he tried tackling this history mystery in a variety of ways, but resolution eluded him. Finally, John, an artist and part-time caterer, solicited the help of *New York Times* reporter Sam Roberts, a customer of his.

At this point, the quest gained momentum. The search for Hinda's death certificate was a straightforward affair, especially since her date of death was known. And the certificate indicated that she had been buried in "Sec. U.H. Ocean View Cemetery" on Staten Island. Case closed, right? Not quite. A call to the cemetery revealed that they had no one of that name buried there. As Sam was later to write, "Mr. Lankenau was confronted not only with a mysterious tombstone, but also a missing body."

Cookbook Hinda?

That's when I received a call. I've had the opportunity to co-sleuth with Sam from time to time and always enjoy it, so when he contacted me about this perplexing gravestone, it was a no-brainer that I would join the hunt. Sam briefed me on the search to date and asked me to find out whatever I could about Hinda.

Like John, I ventured in with a bit of googling, experimenting with versions of her name. Changing the *a* at the end of Hinda to an *e* and the *y* at the end of Amchanitzky to an *i* popped up the Library of Congress entry that John had found previously. Much to my delight, it included the cover of the 1901 cookbook—evidently the first Yiddish language one published in America—featuring a photo of Hinda. Entitled "Manual of How to Cook and Bake," the book included 148 recipes "consumed in the finest Jewish homes in Russia, Galicia, France, England and America." The author claimed that her "45 years' experience in cooking, baking, frying and roasting taught me to prepare all meals very economically," and that the meals "protect children from dyspepsia and other adult diseases."

Now I was even more motivated. Gazing at her face, I thought it was a double injustice that her culinary contributions had been forgotten even before her tombstone had begun its journey. But first I had to determine whether cookbook-Hinda and tombstone-Hinda were indeed the same woman.

Was the mystery woman the one who wrote the first
Yiddish-language cookbook in America?
(Library of Congress)

I hit the usual genealogical databases, but struggled. Amchanitzky is one of those names that can be creatively butchered dozens of ways, and even her first name was subject to distortion, as I learned when I eventually excavated one long-sought record lurking as "Annie Magimity." On the upside, it was a distinctive name and its rarity improved the odds that she was the cookbook author.

It was city directories that finally gave me what I was looking for. Yes, Hinda—*this* Hinda—had been a cook. She and her family ran an "eating house" located at 143 East Broadway, just a mile from where her tombstone would one day materialize on the sidewalk.

Where's Her Family?

So the first part of the mystery was solved. The next task was finding her descendants in the hope that one of them might be able to shed more light on Hinda. This turned out to be no small feat. In addition to the challenges her name posed, there was the matter of her age. In 1910 alone, three sources recorded her age as forty-nine, sixty, and eighty-seven, respectively. Clearly, this was a woman who had her secrets!

Following her family forward in time injected its own complexities as her descendants proved to be quite mobile. Though only a few generations had intervened, I traced them to New York (outside of the city), Massachusetts, California, Illinois, and Florida. And just for giggles, her progeny had Americanized their surname. Dealing with a name like Amchanitzky, I knew to expect that, but it would have been considerate if they had all agreed on a single new name. As it was, I wound up chasing down branches with monikers ranging from Amsher to Shanit.

After pursuing her family as far forward as five generations, I handed over contact information for some living relatives to Sam, who then hit the phone. Most of the descendants had never even heard of Hinda, including a great-great-granddaughter I had located in California. Fortunately, she mentioned Sam's call to her mother, who reminded her that she had her grandfather's journal. Why not take a look? When she did, she tripped across a comment where her grandfather had noted, "father's mother was an excellent cook and she published an excellent cookbook that was sold in New York and Philadelphia." Though we were already confident that Hinda was the writer, it was a bonus to have this confirmation.

But what about the tombstone? No one had any idea.

Cemetery Road Trip

Whenever I get stuck, I go back to the beginning. In this case, that meant the headstone and death certificate. A coworker of my husband's was kind enough to arrange for translation of the stone while I turned my attention to the certificate.

In some respects, it was appropriate that I was working with a journalist because being a genealogist is akin to being a retro-journalist. With a little experience, you learn to question constantly, not take anything at face value, and when possible, go see for yourself. I scoured the document for any clues I had missed the first time around, and as I did, the burial notation caught my eye: "Sec. U.H. Ocean View Cemetery." I knew the cemetery had no record of Hinda, but we seemed to be running out of leads. A quick map check showed that it was about seventy-five miles from my home, and it doesn't take much of an excuse to convince a genealogist to visit a graveyard, so I decided an in-person research jaunt was in order.

The next day, I set the GPS and drove to Ocean View Cemetery on Staten Island. Just as Sam had done, I asked for the plot where Hinda Amchanitzky was buried. And just as had happened with Sam, I was told there was no such person in their records. Strike one.

I was reluctant to give up so easily, so I tried to keep the gentleman behind the counter talking. Without explaining why, I
showed him photos of the tombstone, asking his opinion about
the age—was it typical for 1910 or of more recent vintage? What
kind of granite was it made of? And would he mind taking a look
at the death certificate to see if anything jumped out at him?
When he did, he immediately recognized "Sec. U.H." as an abbreviation for "Section United Hebrew." This, I would later learn,
was a happy coincidence.

When I inquired as to its location within the cemetery, he explained that Ocean View had changed ownership several times,
and that the original was now splintered into several indepen-
dent cemeteries. He suggested I visit the bordering United Hebrew Cemetery.

My hopes soared! Of course Ocean View didn't have the
record. Hinda was now buried in another graveyard that had
been carved out of the first. I hopped back in the car and went to
United Hebrew. For the second time that day, I found myself
chatting with a forty-something man behind the counter and
soon realized that this was to my advantage. It certainly didn't
hurt that I happened to go on this expedition the day before Memorial Day weekend. Since it was already afternoon, everyone I
encountered was in a good mood, anticipating the holiday
ahead. Perhaps that explains why I experienced a feeling of déjà
vu. Then forty-nine years old, it took me a while to recognize
what was happening, but the memory banks finally engaged and
reminded me that this was flirting. Knowing that metropolitan
cemeteries can sometimes be dangerous places (sadly, a favorite
mugging venue for some), I had removed my wedding ring that
day, and the fellows I was dealing with were so pumped about
the long weekend that they were actually flirting with me!

As it turned out, this was very lucky because I would have
otherwise quickly worn out my welcome. Confident I was in the
right place, I asked for Hinda's plot. Crestfallen does not begin to

describe how I felt when I was once again told there was no such record. I had been so certain she was here.

Once again, I shifted into keep-'em-talking mode. Did they, I asked, have any day books? Since I had the date of her burial from her death certificate, might it be possible to look in the business records for the month of May 1910? Sure, came the jovial reply, followed by an office-wide search that turned up every day book *except* the one incorporating May 1910. Strike two.

Becoming more desperate, I recalled that my flirtatious friend had done the initial look-up for Hinda's name on a computer. Could he possibly do a date-based look-up in that same database? He had never tried before, but was game to give it a go. And that's when he found the entry for H. Anachowsky. Yes! She *was* here! Now all I had to do was get her plot details and go take a few photos.

Given that I was at the United Hebrew Cemetery, I was slightly confused when told that she was buried in the section operated by the United Hebrew Community of New York (UHCNY). UHCNY is a society that helps members with burials and other needs, and it was dumb luck for me that it happened to have the same name as the eventual cemetery that took over this portion of the original Ocean View Cemetery. Had the new owners selected any name other than "United Hebrew," the path to Hinda's burial place would have been far more obscured and I could have spent the balance of the day visiting assorted Jewish cemeteries.

Where's the Plot?

With plot details in hand, I drove out to the UHCNY section and found it quite large. The fellow in the office had been vague about where the plot would be situated, but I wasn't concerned because I had the coordinates—row and grave number—and had done this in countless burial grounds before.

It was only then that I appreciated for the first time that I was looking for something that probably wasn't there. Unless the tombstone that found its way to Manhattan was a replacement for an earlier one (or an earlier one that had been replaced), I was seeking a patch of grass. How would I know when I had the right spot?

I wandered back and forth through the section and tried counting out rows and graves sites, but nothing seemed to fit. I finally settled on what I thought was the most likely location, but still uncertain, jotted down details from the flanking tombstones. Returning to the office, I asked if I could impose yet again by seeing if they could find person X and person Y, Hinda's possible neighbors in eternal repose, in their database. Hoping for confirmation, I cringed when it became clear that these two were nowhere near Hinda. I could feel strike three stalking me.

Pushing my flirting rights to the limit, I inquired whether the database could be searched in such a way as to identify who was in the plots next to Hinda. That one stumped the band, but just then, the president—who had been at the cemetery back when the database was developed—walked in and overheard the conversation. A few keystrokes later, and I had what I needed. Better yet, he pulled out a map of the UHCNY section that clarified the root of my confusion. At one time, men and women had been buried separately and in chronological order (so much for being buried near loved ones!), but over time, later interspersed burials had blurred the gender and date lines, making it harder to find specific graves.

This information made it easy for me to detect Hinda's plot the next time out. I simply went to the women's area and looked for a cluster of tombstones with a heavy sprinkling of 1910 death dates. Walking that vicinity, I soon spied Hinda's neighbors with her in between. As expected, there was no headstone, though I could feel a slight depression in the earth where it had once been. Closely inspecting the other stones, I saw that Hinda's was their contemporary. The material, lettering, mix of language, and other nuances all resembled those of other 1910-era stones.

Hinda's Stone Goes Home

While I was busy finding relatives and exploring cemeteries, Sam continued to follow the trail of the tombstone and was able to determine that the recently sold building John had found it in front of once housed an artists' collective and burial society. Digging deeper, he learned that it had been given to the founders of that society by a fellow artist who rescued it when he saw construction workers dumping granite slabs from a nearby building that once had a monument maker in the basement. How and why Hinda's gravestone made the initial trip from Staten Island to the monument maker in Manhattan remains unknown.

Perhaps one day the missing leg of the tombstone's travels will be uncovered, but what's most important is that—thanks to John's custodianship, a bit of detective work, and the Center for Jewish History (which happens to be digitizing historic cookbooks and paid to have the monument re-installed)—both Hinda's tombstone and memory were finally restored in 2010, one hundred years after her passing.

CHAPTER TWENTY

Grandma Stepped Out

My accidental genetic discovery

IN JUNIOR HIGH, I was in the chess club. My electives in high school were Latin (*rana in urna mea est!*) and Probability and Statistics. And for no particular reason, I have a pair of master's degrees, including one in information technology from Johns Hopkins. I'm no Temperance Brennan, but I definitely know how to get my geek on. So it was no surprise to anyone who knows me when I started playing with DNA about a decade ago.

Whether people realize it or not, we're already in the early days of the genomics revolution. Move over, information age, there's a new revolution in town! And what makes this one stand apart from its predecessors is that it's the first in which average Joes can participate. Though many are still learning about the availability of consumer DNA tests, the first genetic genealogy companies launched back in 2000, so for the past ten years, hundreds of thousands of us have been quietly swabbing, swishing, and spitting in an attempt to learn more about our roots. In fact, some "civilians" are so gung-ho that they could almost be described as nags to the scientific community, constantly campaigning for more sophisticated tests, standardization of reporting, and greater effort to uncover ancestrally informative markers.

I joined this group of early-bird customers in 2001, largely due to my work with the army. Since I was already tracking down relatives of soldiers from past conflicts to provide DNA reference samples for identification purposes, I understood how these tests could be used to shed light on our family and heritage. That's why I was one of the first in line, shouting, "Ooh! Ooh! Me! Me!"

My Genetic Baby Steps

My first foray into the genetic world involved my unusual surname. All Smolenyaks in the world can trace their roots to the village of Osturna in present-day Slovakia. There were four Smolenyak families from the village and since we had all lived within a thirty-house distance of each other for centuries, it seemed reasonable to conclude that we shared a common ancestor. But the local church had burned down in the 1790s, so I couldn't push back any earlier to find the connections.

The first commercial test that became available was Y-DNA, which is passed from father to son down through the generations—much the same way surnames usually travel through time. When this became available, I rounded up four Smolenyak males, one from each of the four families, to test. I just knew that they would all share the same paternal, genetic signature so I could finally prove that we were all related. Wrong.

None of the four matched each other. In fact, none of us were even close. My theory was completely wrong. Being a Smolenyak both by birth and by marriage (beat them odds!), I suppose I should have been pleased, but truthfully, this wasn't the outcome I had hoped for. Still, it excited me about the possibilities of genetic genealogy. Within six weeks, I had been able to answer a question that had been eating at me for years—one that the paper trail never could have settled.

Recognizing the potential, I became an early proponent of DNA testing as a supplement to conventional genealogy, but I wasn't exactly greeted with open arms. In fact, it took two years to get anyone to accept an article or talk on the topic. But gradually, resistance began to fade as people realized that this was not meant as some sort of genealogical shortcut, but rather, another tool to help us unlock the past. I like to think I had something to do with this as I've spent the last decade crisscrossing the country speaking about the topic to anyone who would listen and coauthored (with Ann Turner, M.D.) *Trace Your Roots with DNA*, a book many diving into genetic genealogy cut their teeth on.

Auto-What?

Because I frequently speak and write about genetic genealogy, I feel an obligation to take just about every kind of test offered by every company in the industry. I've missed a few over the years, but my poor father has been tested so many times (as a female, I have no Y-chromosome, so I borrow my father's DNA as a proxy) that he doesn't even ask questions. He just swabs and says he "hopes it's doing some good."

Whenever a new kind of test emerges, I feel an additional obligation to test the tester. I did this out of the shoot with my Smolenyak experiment and have continued to do so over the years. After a decade, so many of my relatives have taken so many different kinds of tests from so many companies that I believed I had nothing left to learn genetically. But once again I was wrong.

A few years ago, a new type of autosomal testing was introduced. Up until then, we had been dealing with Y-DNA, which told us about our direct, paternal lines, and mtDNA, which informed us about our direct, maternal lines. While these tests forced us into a branch-at-a-time mode of exploring our family trees, we were fairly content because this was more than we had before which was—well, nothing.

We all dreamed, however, of an autosomal test that could give us a sense of the entire tree. In fact, there was one for a few years, but it didn't take much kicking of the tires to realize that it was flawed. The company that offered it eventually went out of business (though I'm disappointed to say that some have since licensed the technology and resurrected this misleading test, but consumers will wise up and I assume it will once again vanish).

Finally, our wish was granted. In November of 2007, 23andMe.com in California introduced an autosomal test dubbed Relative Finder. Perhaps six months later, Family Tree DNA in Texas would offer a similar product called Family Finder. Both were autosomal tests that could give us an idea of our continental heritage—that is, provide a breakdown of our roots as being approximately X percent European, Y percent African, and Z percent Asian. But what most of us found far more compelling was the test's ability to help us find previously unknown relatives.

Testing the Tester

Supposedly, if I were to take this new type of autosomal test, the company would be able to highlight anyone in its database who was some sort of cousin of mine (in case you're wondering, privacy walls were put in place so no one would have to deal with unwanted cousins). The tests purported to be able to detect relatives as distantly related as tenth cousins, although the companies were quite clear that the accuracy dropped dramatically after perhaps the fourth or fifth cousin level. Still, how many of us can name even all of our third cousins? As far as I was concerned, anything beyond that point would be a bonus.

Think about this for a moment. Assuming it works, the power of this kind of testing comes largely from the size of the databases. The more people tested, the more potential cousins in the databases for the company's algorithms to pluck out for each of us. And over time, as more people jump in, we'll all learn about more cousins. Fast-forward, say, a decade, and an adoptee who has no clue whatsoever about his or her heritage could take one of these tests and instantly learn about dozens (or hundreds) of cousins. If you take the time to let this sink in, it's pretty darn amazing.

I wanted to believe, but as is my custom when a new genetic technology emerges, I decided to test the tester. Assuming optimistically that this would work, I mentally fast-forwarded and pondered how I might be able to explain this to my audiences. With that in mind, I developed an experiment. I rounded up fifteen people to test, but fifteen deliberately chosen people.

First, all of them had roots in Osturna, the village that was the source of all the Smolenyaks now scattered around the world. This place is still the end of the road today, and historically has been quite isolated, so I theorized that many of us might be related in ways that the paper trail hadn't yet brought to light.

Second, I picked particular individuals for their degree of relationship to me and each other. Though I've been speaking in terms of cousins, the tests could also spot more closely related people such as parents and siblings, so I tested not only myself, but also my father, sister, and a nephew. Then I set about methodically approaching a first cousin, a second cousin, a third cousin, and so forth to join my project. I wanted to see how accurate the company was in predicting relationships and this seemed a logical way to go about it. Would it really recognize my father as my parent? Would it be able to distinguish a first cousin from a second? Could it tell if any of the Osturnites were related to each other in various ways? This is what I was aiming for.

A Minor Hiccup

Since I've been doing this kind of thing for so long, my family—including my more distant cousins—are used to me asking for genetic samples, so they kindly humor me. Even if they're not that interested themselves, they'll often participate for my sake. Thanks to my good-natured kin, I didn't have any difficulty persuading the appropriate people to test—with one exception.

I was purposely testing Osturnites, people who might have some overlap with the paternal half of my family tree, because I hoped to find some unknown relationships with and among them. But on the paternal side of my family, I only have one cousin, and he's not keen on DNA testing. I respect this so when I occasionally encounter this perspective, I back off. But this cousin's non-participation would leave a hole in my tidy experiment. What to do?

My uncle, this cousin's father, has led a colorful life. I won't bore you with details. Suffice it to say that when a stranger contacted me out of the blue claiming to be another child of this uncle, I suspected it might be true. When a second person—completely unconnected to the first—reached out to me with the same story a short while later, I started wondering how many cousins I might have.

If you live in the genealogy world, you hear stories of this nature all the time. You may, for instance, remember Oprah's discovery of a half sister when she was fifty-six and the sister was forty-seven. Families keep secrets, but sooner or later, they tend to spill. So these sudden cousins didn't particularly phase me, but I was curious. Were they really my cousins?

If you're related to me, I'm going to ask you to take a DNA test, so when these alleged cousins contacted me, I did just that. And then I forgot about it. Rather fortuitously, one of them called me as I was orchestrating my genetic experiment to tell me he had decided to take a test. Perfect timing! Better yet, if my uncle really was his father, I'd have a first cousin to plug the gap left by the cousin I had grown up with and known about all my life.

The Envelope, Please

Though the testing only took about a month, it seemed a long time before the results began to trickle in, but when they did, I was impressed. Just as I had postulated, there were countless relationships among the fifteen Osturnites. My husband, in fact, turned out to be related to all of the fourteen other Osturnites who participated, including me! The earlier Y-DNA testing had indicated that in spite of marrying a fellow Smolenyak, I had failed to marry my cousin—but now autosomal testing showed that we were related, but on some other, non-Smolenyak branch. I suppose I should be grateful that I was the most distant of his relatives, designated as roughly his tenth cousin.

Taking a closer look, I spot-checked some of the various Osturna cousinships that had surfaced. I like to think that it merits a line on my geek résumé to have all the church and census records for my village of origin back to the 1790s at the ready to consult whenever needed. Sure, they're in a mix of Latin, Hungarian, and the Cyrillic alphabet, but that's half the fun! I was very pleased when I was able to use these records to confirm several of the genetically indicated relationships that fell within the last two hundred years.

But what about the other part of my experiment? How accurate had the company been in ascertaining the known relationships I had deliberately incorporated? I went to my own results and started clicking away. Father? Check. Sister? Check. Nephew? Check again. How about the relationship between my father and nephew? Yup, nailed that too.

I gradually worked my way through all the relatives I had seeded my experiment with and was dazzled by the accuracy.

This stuff really worked! Well, almost. There was one aberration that gave me pause.

Occam's Razor

When the last-minute, alleged cousin joined the project, I expected one of two outcomes: either he would appear as my first cousin or not at all. What I was not prepared for was to see him designated as a second cousin.

This made no sense. On the one hand, he was clearly related to me and quite closely. He wasn't some random stranger. This fellow and I (and my father, sister, nephew) all shared a healthy chunk of our genetic makeup. Why, then, was he showing as my second cousin instead of my first? Up until this point, all the results had lined up as expected, and I couldn't understand how this testing could capture more distant relationships accurately, while getting this one wrong.

Trying to understand, I poked around a little more and saw that the test results also included paternal haplogroups. A haplogroup can be regarded as a deep ancestry perspective of your direct paternal line, and tells you which branch of the world's paternal family tree you descend from. I knew from previous testing that my father was I2b. If this cousin was my uncle's son, he should also be I2b since my dad, his brother, and any male children of both of them would all share a common male ancestor. So I was doubly perplexed when this fellow turned up as R1a.

By now, I was genuinely confounded. I racked my brains for any scenario that could make sense of all this and came up with crazy notions involving a great-uncle's son passed off as his sister's child and other such unlikely situations. Deciding I needed to talk through it, I called my sister and started to explain.

I'm a big believer in Occam's Razor, the concept that all things being equal, the simplest explanation is usually the correct one.

I was babbling to my sister about assorted possibilities and suddenly blurted, "The only way this could all make sense is if Grandma stepped out."

It Couldn't Be

I know that in a Maury Povich kind of world, this sounds less than earth-shattering, so let me try to put into perspective how improbable this seemed. My grandmother was born in this country, but barely. Her parents had arrived from Ukraine just a few years earlier. Her father was a coal miner and a nasty fellow. It took decades of research, but I eventually learned that he was a bigamist, having left behind a wife before coming to America. He married my great-grandmother a mere seven weeks after arriving, and after six children, would kill her in a drunken rage.

My grandmother was the oldest daughter of this troubled union, and had to take over her mother's responsibilities while also scrubbing office floors to help support the family. She graduated into young adulthood around the time of the Great Depression, and though she died in 1980, I still remember the cabinets she stocked with canned goods in case hardship should circle back around and the plastic covers she protected her furniture with so it would last. She was five-foot-nothing and stockily built, and in spite of having spent her whole life in Pennsylvania and New Jersey, slipped into a strange language whenever she didn't want us to understand what she was talking about. She was, in short, as old country as one could be living in the New World and always bracing herself for the worst to happen—an American babushka.

By this point, I had been researching the family for decades and playing with DNA for seven. I had peeled back many secrets in my family's past including most of what I just described, so I truly thought I knew it all. The last thing I would have ever expected was that my grandmother had a son with a man other than my grandfather, but had it been anyone else's family or grandmother, I knew that the conclusion would have been obvious to me.

If true, this would explain why this newfound cousin didn't share the same paternal haplogroup as my father. And since he and I would only have one grandparent in common—making us only half as related as we had thought—it would explain why he had shown up as my second cousin instead of my first.

I was still incredulous, but realized that I had set myself up perfectly to analyze the situation due to the people I had selected to test. Working with the hypothesis that Grandma's two sons had different fathers, I calculated what the relationship should be between the new cousin and each of the other people I tested, or whether there should be any relationship at all. Everything now fit perfectly. Grandma had indeed stepped out.

Breaking the News

My accidental genetic discovery left me with a conundrum: what should I tell my father? Should I tell him that his only brother was really his half brother or just let it be? I mulled this over for perhaps a month until chatting with my father on the phone one day. Not able to keep it in anymore, I abruptly asked, "Dad, if I were to stumble across something unsettling about the family, would you want to know?" He instantly replied "yes," so I told him.

I was tremendously relieved when he took it in stride, soon suggesting that this might explain why his brother had been the only one in the family to ever have asthma. It was interesting to him, but not hurtful. Luckily for me, this pattern of acceptance repeated itself as I gradually informed the others. Each time I trotted out my "unsettling" question. No one declined and no one was upset.

Of course, all of this raised another question: who was my

uncle's father? I have to consider all the possibilities ranging from an affair to assault. Frankly, I'd prefer to think it was the former, but it bears remembering that times were different seventy-plus years ago and victims were often made to feel ashamed as if they were somehow responsible. But hoping that my grandmother had an *affaire de coeur*, I have embarked on my next experiment trying to determine my uncle's paternity.

How exactly am I doing this? I'm using Y-DNA testing at Family Tree DNA to find an answer. I had the newfound cousin's Y-DNA tested to serve as a baseline, and while I might get lucky one day and spot a match in the database, it turns out that his paternal genetic signature is quite rare. So far, he has no matches or anyone close.

Always the impatient sort, I'm developing theories to test. The R1a result mentioned earlier suggests that I'm looking for someone of Slavic origin and my grandmother's circle of acquaintances wasn't that extensive, so I'm digging through my memory banks coming up with names of men I met in the company of my grandparents (it's so often a family friend, isn't it?). Could it have been that man who told me as a child that his mustache (I had never seen one before) was a toothbrush he kept handy at all times?

Of course, the likely candidates are all deceased now, so I'm tracking down their male descendants, and as you might imagine, having some peculiar conversations over the phone trying to persuade strangers to take DNA tests. You might be surprised to hear that no one has hung up on me—probably because they're as intrigued with the notion of tripping across an unexpected uncle or cousin as most of us would be.

As I write these words, the first test is under way. I'm not holding my breath that I'll get it right on the first try, but with some patience, I expect to eventually identify my uncle's father. For better or worse, the notion of taking your secrets to the grave is now quaint. Sorry, Grandma, it was an accident!

CHAPTER TWENTY-ONE

They Call Me Yak-Yak

*What I learned from assisting the FBI
with civil rights cold cases*

IF YOU HAD TOLD ME that I would one day meet with the FBI in the parking lot of the local burrito joint, I would have scoffed at your wild imagination—that is, until it happened. When the call came to rendezvous, I was mystified but intrigued. There was no way I wasn't going.

I pulled up in the designated spot and scanned my mirrors repeatedly, and then, just like in the movies, a car with darkened windows pulled up beside me. Two agents got out with paperwork they asked me to sign with the code name I had been given: *Yak-Yak.* Ah yes, echoes of distant recess taunts—the play on my last name, Smolenyak. Perhaps I shouldn't divulge this name here, but no one insisted that I keep it to myself, and frankly, I'm tickled. (But if this is a federal faux-pas and I've just blown my cover, I take full responsibility and will gladly dream up several no-one-will-ever-guess alternatives.)

Civil Rights Cold Cases

My journey to that parking lot began several months earlier with a press release about the Civil Rights Era Cold Case Initiative. This partnership is a joint effort by the FBI, civil rights groups, and federal, state, and local law enforcement agencies to "reassess . . . unsolved or inadequately solved racially motivated homicides from the civil rights era." Though some might think that investigating decades-old cases is an exercise in futility, Director Robert S. Mueller noted at the 2007 launch that recent successes had "restored our hope and renewed our resolve." He added, "We cannot turn back the clock. We cannot right these wrongs. But we can try to bring a measure of justice to those who remain."

The press release that caught my eye was issued on the second anniversary of the initiative and included a list of names and circumstances of victims' deaths. About a third of the targeted cases had encountered difficulty due to "the passage of time and the migration of many families." While experience had shown that relatives and witnesses are often more willing to talk now (one agent remarked, "Some are relieved to talk after forty years and get it off their chest"), the challenge was finding surviving family members and others with information about the crimes. That's what the FBI hoped to accomplish by sharing names, dates, and locations of deaths publicly.

I eyeballed the summaries and realized that I could help. The very same skill set I apply when researching cases for the army or assorted coroners' offices was relevant here. Start with a few tidbits of information from the 1950s or '60s and try to locate the next-of-kin today? I'm your girl.

John Earl Reese

It wasn't what I had planned when I began work that day, but seeing this list made me put aside my own to-do list, and it was

John Earl Reese I selected first. The just-the-facts-ma'am rendi-
tion provided by the FBI was brief, but riveting:

> On October 22, 1955, John Earl Reese, a 16-year-old
> African-American male was shot and killed by two men
> who fired several rounds into a predominantly African-
> American café in Gregg County, Texas. Two other
> African-American females were shot, but survived the
> attack.

Sixteen years old. Somebody's child in 1955. And at the time I
was researching his case, someone who by all rights should have
been a sixty-nine-year-old grandfather.

Texas is one of the better states to research due to the availability of several vital records indexes. A death index for the state
had been online for years, but was skimpy in terms of details.
Just around the time of this press release, though, digitized images of some of these records had recently been uploaded to the
Internet. Equipped with the details furnished by the FBI, it took
just minutes to retrieve John Reese's death certificate.

I scrutinized it as I always do because such records often hold
many clues. The first thing that jumped out was that he was
born on October 9th, coincidentally my birthday as well. Perhaps
that was why I had been drawn to his case? Sadly, this meant
that John was barely sixteen, having celebrated his birthday just
two weeks prior to his murder. Reinforcing his youth was his occupation given as "school boy." But it was his cause of death that
grabbed my attention:

Gunshot wound
with Fractured skull
(accidental)

How could firing several rounds into a local hangout be accidental? My husband's father spent most of his life with a limp

because his brother shot one of his legs during some horseplay back in a time when we were far more lax about gun safety. *That* was an accidental shooting. But this was a teenager who had been shot—along with two others—on a Saturday night out. There were *several rounds* involved. I struggled to think of any kind of scenario in which that could have been accidental, but it simply didn't compute.

So began my education. Sure, I knew about the civil rights movement, but even though I had lived through some of it, I was so young that I thought of it as somewhat historical—something I learned about in school. Just as it's hard for me to fathom that my grandmothers weren't born with the right to vote, it was difficult to wrap my head around the reality that racism, particularly by law enforcement, could be so blatant. I didn't know at the time, but John's cause of death would push my education still further the following year.

Finding the Family

Shifting my attention back to the certificate, I sighed when I saw his parents' names: John T. Reese and Katherine Brown. Mention names like Smith, Jones, and Williams to a roomful of genealogists and you're guaranteed a collective groan. We're not fond of common names—ones that will make us wade through countless candidates rather than flit directly to the person of interest. Brown is the fifth most popular surname in the United States, and Reese, while less common, isn't rare. First names like John and Katherine weren't going to help narrow the field, but at least John's father included the middle initial *T.* Middle initials can sometimes be a genealogist's best friend (often a tiebreaker among various contenders), so I was grateful. Also recorded were John's birth place (Gregg County) and that of his parents (Rusk County). A quick map check revealed that the two counties bordered each other. So the family was more or less local and had been for some time. That boded well since it meant I wasn't dealing with a moving target.

I decided to try to get traction on John's father, but John Reese is such a common name that it wasn't possible to readily spot him in statewide and national indexes. There were just too many men who shared the same name, but ultimately, I was able to ferret out a county-level index (an iffy prospect, but worth checking) that showed that John T. Reese died in 1986 in Gregg County. The same tactics failed to turn up his mother and intensive massaging of birth indexes similarly thwarted my efforts to identify likely siblings. Typical. One step forward and two steps back.

Returning my focus to the father, I used the details found in the county death index to back into his entry in the Social Security Death Index (a database of most Americans who have died since 1962, as well as a smattering of those who died earlier). This gave his birth date in 1914. From his son's death certificate, I knew that John T. had been born in Rusk County, so armed with his birth date, I looked for earlier traces of him in that area. After finding his WWII army enlistment record showing him as married in 1943, I had a go at 1930 and 1920 census records, hoping to obtain the names of his parents and siblings who would be enumerated in the same household. And there he was. Right name (complete with middle initial of T), right age, right place. There was only one fellow who matched these criteria in Rusk County in 1930 and 1920.

Now I had the names of his siblings. Contemplating my options, I selected his youngest sister because the odds were good that she would be alive. Brothers would have been easier to follow forward through time since they wouldn't have married into another surname, but I knew that the Texas birth indexes were flexible enough to often include mothers' maiden names. Hedging my bets that she had stayed in the area, I restricted my search to Gregg County and spotted what I suspected were five children born to this sister. Any lingering doubts I might have had evaporated when I noticed that she had named one of her sons Alvin after her father, shortly after he had passed away. This little tribute to her father amounted to a genealogical tell and assured me I had the right woman.

From the birth indexes, I had learned her married name, so now it was a matter of finding her in one of any of a few dozen people-finding websites. While these resources are frequently out of date, I figured that if anyone could find her current contact information, it would be the FBI! So I snagged what I had learned about John's aunt and decided I was ready to submit it to the FBI.

Hello, FBI?

Hmmm . . . submit to the FBI. How exactly was I supposed to do that? I revisited the press release that had prompted this search and saw that it instructed the reader to contact their local FBI office. It dawned on me that aside from childhood field trips to the headquarters in Washington, D.C., I had had zero interaction with the FBI during my life. I googled around a bit and was surprised to find that there was a branch office about five miles away from where I live in New Jersey, so I picked up the phone. The agent who responded was gracious, but perplexed. She hadn't heard of this initiative, but she'd look into it. Taking my name and number, she said they'd get back to me. Right.

I figured at that point that I might have done this for nothing, but just ten minutes later, the phone rang. It was the office in Philadelphia wondering whether I could please e-mail the information I had found. I marveled at the efficiency, still not quite believing I was dealing with the FBI—something I had no inkling of doing when I woke up that morning.

At this point, I could have whipped out an e-mail in mere moments, but given my experience courting coroners and medical examiners, I thought I had better take the time—especially with this first case—to spell out how I had reached the conclusions I had. I outlined my logic and process, much as I've done here, but included more specifics and image captures of relevant documents. I wanted them to feel confident in my findings.

On the Case

And they were. I tackled a few additional cases, thus beginning my entirely unexpected association with the FBI. As it happens, this was also roughly the time I began helping NCIS. (The real one, not the one on TV!) That relationship developed through word of mouth. One of the coroners' offices I had dealt with recommended me to a police department that had cause to occasionally work in conjunction with NCIS. Before long, NCIS began contacting me directly for assistance on cold cases—locating victims, witnesses, and others somehow connected to crimes that occurred decades ago. I continue to do what I can because it gives me great satisfaction to use the skills I've honed over the years for purposes like this.

None of this was deliberate, but it's a fortuitous evolution that I've welcomed and decided to share in a Cold Cases talk I developed primarily for family history audiences. It was at one of these that I gained fresh insight into why this research is so critical. I delivered the lecture to a group of perhaps 300 people in Southern California, and included the case of John Earl Reese in addition to several others. As I've done here, I shared my reaction to the hard-to-swallow cause of death.

The talk went well, and as generally happens, a cluster of folks gathered around to ask more questions after it was over. Among them was a tall gentleman with a stately bearing and an angry expression. I soon learned why. He identified himself as a retired police officer from Texas and had something important to ask. Did it ever occur to me, he asked, that John Reese could have fractured his skull by cracking it on the back of his chair?

I was momentarily stunned into silence, thinking I had misheard. The others standing around also went quiet. I had said nothing about whether John was sitting or standing and made no reference to chairs or other furniture. I couldn't have since I had no clue myself. And yet, decades later sitting in the audience at a genealogical conference, this officer had felt compelled to conjure up a scenario in an attempt to rationalize the "accidental" cause of death. I was unable to refrain from responding, "If that happened, do you think it might have had something to do with a bullet entering his head?"

I fully understand that this man is not representative of the vast majority of officers of the law then or now, and I admittedly could have been more artful in responding to him, but this exchange opened my eyes. Until that moment, I hadn't grasped the realities that enveloped John Earl Reese and all the other civil rights victims. If that mind-set still existed in some in 2010, what must it have been like in 1955? Now, finally, I was beginning to understand.

Were I to encounter this fellow again, I would thank him. It wasn't his intention, but he seriously schooled—and motivated—me that day. I couldn't wait to get to my next case.

CHAPTER TWENTY-TWO

Annie Moore, Ellis Island's First

Rectifying a case of historical identity theft

I WOULD HAVE RAISED a skeptical brow if you had told me in 2002 that an Irish lass by the name of Annie Moore would consume endless hours (and quite a few pennies) of mine over the next decade. Like any Irish American proud of her roots, I knew who she was—the first to arrive at Ellis Island, making her the poster child of immigration, and by proxy, the American dream. Representative also of the Irish diaspora, this teenager is an accidental but genuine symbol of two nations, which is why I think she matters and should be one of those historical tidbits that every schoolchild masters. But I had no inkling then how she would insinuate herself into my life. Nor did I realize how her story would abruptly sprout a fresh chapter each time I thought we had reached the end.

I'm not going to tell her entire story here because to do so would require its own book, but I thought I'd share a digest version of her rediscovery and then dwell a bit on the latest episode in Annie's ongoing saga.

A Case of Mistaken Identity

Annie Moore died in Manhattan in 1924 at the age of fifty. I say this with certainty because history was corrected several years ago. Until then, a native-born American had been passing for her. How did this happen? We were careless with our history.

Annie arrived at Ellis Island from Ireland with her younger brothers, Anthony and Philip, on January 1, 1892, and as the first to alight at the newly opened immigration station, was greeted with much fanfare and made headlines in all the newspapers of the day. Then we promptly forgot her—that is, until the restoration of this national landmark got under way almost a century after her arrival and she reemerged in statue form at both Ellis Island and the Cobh Heritage Centre in Cork.

Her proud descendants naturally claimed her, so her post-Ellis story and photo found its way into books, museums, and documentaries. Annie had finally recovered her little piece of history. There was just one problem with this happy ending: history had reclaimed the wrong Annie.

Family lore tends to be accepted at face value and the family in question had fallen prey to an elderly relative's wishful thinking. Due to her stories, they thought they were related to Ellis Island Annie, but they were actually descended from another woman of the same name who was born in Illinois. What's strange about this is that no one bothered to check, so the wrong Annie's story was allowed to seep into the cracks of history.

Fast-forward to 2002. I detected the discrepancy while working on a PBS documentary called *They Came to America*, and informed those I assumed would be interested. Four years passed and the wrong Annie's tale continued to circulate. Visiting the American National Tree exhibit at the National Constitution Center in Philadelphia in 2006, I spotted a photo of the imposter and decided that something had to be done. True, she had only accidentally usurped Annie's place, but still, the real Annie deserved to have her story known.

The True Annie

Recognizing that I was dealing with a needle in a haystack situation (you'd be stunned to know how many Irish-born Annie Moores were running around New York at the time), I enlisted the help of my fellow genealogists by launching a contest offering $1,000 for the first proof of the real Annie. Genealogists can't resist a mystery, so just six weeks later, my husband and I found ourselves standing at the site of her unmarked grave in Calvary Cemetery in Queens. After tracking down her descendants—her great-niece Pat Somerstein having been instrumental in providing the critical clue for finding the others—I organized a family reunion in New York, which morphed into a press conference when journalist Sam Roberts shared Annie's true story on the front page of the *New York Times*.

So now we had Annie's story right. Well, almost. The newspapers that covered her arrival all remarked on the coincidence of it being her fifteenth birthday, and even today, this "fact" is widely reported. But thanks to the efforts of Tim McCoy's eleven-year-old students from Scoil Oilibhéir in Cork, we learned a short while later that Annie was born in May and was really seventeen years old. While making a film about her, fittingly titled *From Cork to New York*, they found her birth and baptismal records in the hometown they share with Annie. In all likelihood, some officials involved in the 1892 opening of Ellis Island realized the PR value of their first arrival being a charming birthday girl, and it took twenty-first-century Irish schoolchildren to correct their fiction!

Two years later, her descendants organized a memorial dedication for Annie at Calvary Cemetery. It was an impressive event attended by several hundred people including Ronan Tynan, the Irish tenor who belted out "Isle of Hope, Isle of Tears," a much-beloved song about Annie, and the song's composer, Brendan Graham, who had traveled from Ireland just for the ceremony. The evening before, Tim McCoy, who had emerged as Annie's protector on the other side of the pond, had orchestrated an event in Cork to install a historical marker on the last home Annie lived in before coming to America.

In between the film made by the Irish schoolchildren and the commemorative events in Cork and New York, theater artist Alia Faith Williams wrote and produced a wonderful play about Annie cleverly called *Making Up History* (with "up" squeezed in as if a correction). I had the privilege of attending and was blown away. And most recently, the Cobh Heritage Centre in Cork has named its educational resources room for Annie.

I couldn't have been happier that Annie was finally getting her due. Statues, a memorial, and a plaque now marked the places associated with her life, and her story was being told in song and film, on stage, and in a research facility named for her. What more could I wish for?

Photo Fishing

There was one more thing—a photo. Since 2006, when the real Annie had come to light, I had hoped to find an image of her. Relatives remembered having seen one, but no one knew where it might be and were afraid it had slipped out of family hands when Gerry Donovan, the last of Annie's descendants to live on the Lower East Side of Manhattan, had passed away in 2001. I kept nagging, but to no avail. So imagine my surprise when her great-granddaughter, Maureen Peterson, handed me the photo on the next page after Annie's memorial service.

Astounded, I stared at it and asked the obvious question: Was this Annie at Ellis Island with her brothers Anthony and Philip? If so, it would be one of those iconic images that should pop up in every American history textbook. This, it turned out, was what Maureen was hoping I could tell her. Michael Shulman, Philip's grandson and Annie's great-nephew, found it at—of all places— the Ellis Island library. Well, that was definitely a point in its

Could this be Annie and her brothers arriving at Ellis Island?
(Bob Hope Memorial Library at Ellis Island)

favor! So just as I thought my Annie adventure was winding down, the next phase began.

The best way to determine whether this was really Annie and her brothers was to find other photos to compare to this one, so I begged her descendants to please have another look. It took some time, but a few months later, not one, but two family photographs of Annie surfaced! More significantly, they came independently from separate branches of her family. Great-niece Pat Somerstein and great-granddaughter Maureen Peterson each found one—one from the late 1890s, perhaps six or seven years after her arrival, and the other probably taken within a few years of her death at age fifty. Neither Pat nor Maureen knew at the time of the other photo's existence, and yet, they both had the same handwriting on the back identifying her as "Mama Schayer" (Annie's married name).

Unfortunately, we had no such luck with Anthony and Philip. Anthony died young and there had been a house fire in Philip's

line, resulting in the loss of family pictures of him. Though assorted cousins were located and contacted, no other images of
Philip have been found to date.

Still, I was elated that we now had two confirmed photographs
of Annie! It was wonderful to finally know what she looked like,
and the resemblance between the older woman in these images
and the girl at Ellis Island was hard to miss. Her descendants
could have come back with pictures of a blond, of a willowy
woman, of someone with pointy features, squinty eyes, generous
lips, or any of a million other distinguishing characteristics that
would have instantly dismissed the notion that the girl at Ellis
Island was Annie. But instead, I found myself gazing at what
appeared to be older versions of her.

Photo Finish

New York Times reporter Sam Roberts had gotten wind of the
fact that photos of Annie had been located, so he contacted me
asking about them. I excitedly told him about all three and suggested he get in contact with representatives at Ellis Island to
comment on the one in their possession.

I explained that Michael Shulman had found it in a collection
donated to the library by the grandson of John B. Weber, the first
superintendent of Ellis Island. This provenance was significant
since Weber was the one who, according to all the news articles
at the time, had presented Annie with a $10 gold coin. The two
had indisputably met on January 1,1892. Furthermore, he had
only served at Ellis Island until April 1893, which considerably
narrowed the time frame for any photographs that might have
been in his collection. Michael told me that it was one of only a
few images in the album that was unlabeled, but given the importance of the opening day of Ellis Island to the owner, he may
have felt that its contents were beyond forgetting.

I was dumbfounded when Roberts informed me a short while later that Ellis Island denied that it was Annie and her brothers. Asked how they knew, they said that the photo had been taken at the Barge Office. The Barge Office, based in Battery Park, had served as a temporary immigrant processing center while Ellis Island was being constructed, so I acknowledged that it was plausible due to the timing involved. Curiously, though, no substantiation was given for the claim that it was the Barge Office, so I remained unconvinced and decided to dig deeper.

Let's Start at the Very Beginning . . .

Going back to square one, I summarized what I knew for sure:

- The photo shows three children of the correct genders and approximate ages to be Annie and her brothers.
- The girl looked strikingly similar to Annie in later years as verified though two independently sourced photos.
- The photograph belonged to the first superintendent of Ellis Island who had definitely greeted Annie upon her arrival.
- This same man only worked at Ellis Island until April 1893.

So far, so good. Then I racked my brain for any ways I could prove or disprove that the photo was Annie and her brothers or that it was taken at the Barge Office. What follows are the approaches I used:

- I revisited the photograph of the three children seeking any additional features or factors that could be used to support or refute the location or the event, and obtained

high-resolution copies of every page of the album in
which the photo was discovered to look for any additional
context or clues.

- Hoping to find any images of the interior of the Barge
  Office or the original Ellis Island (which burned to the
  ground in 1897), as well as any depictions or descriptions of Annie at the time of her arrival, I scoured online resources such as newspaper databases, resulting in
  the purchase of several original issues of magazines
  from the 1890s. My husband and I conducted research
  at the New York Public Library scrolling through every
  newspaper we could find for articles about the opening
  of Ellis Island, while my sister and I performed similar
  research at the National Archives in College Park. I have
  subsequently hired other genealogists to consult with
  photo and newspaper experts at the New York Public Library (I wanted to be sure I hadn't overlooked anything), the Library of Congress, and at the Harry
  Ransom Center of the University of Texas (for the *New
  York Journal American* photo morgue housed there). I
  also reached out to the genealogical community for assistance in this regard.

- I asked Maureen Taylor, described by the *Wall Street Journal* as "the nation's foremost historical photo detective,"
  to examine and analyze the images.

- I commissioned renowned forensic artist Stephen Man-
  cusi, a twenty-seven-year veteran of the New York City
  Police Department and chairman of the International
  Association for Identification's Forensic Certification
  Board, to conduct a facial image comparison between the
  later, confirmed photos of Annie and the girl standing be-
  tween the two boys in the photograph found at Ellis
  Island. Not wishing to lead the witness, I cropped Annie

from the one in question and provided him no context, so he would have no idea when doing his analysis of the Ellis Island connection.

- I tracked down descendants of John B. Weber, original owner of the photograph being studied, to see if others might be available for comparison. I also located relatives of Patrick McCool, an immigration agent with the Mission of Our Lady of the Rosary, who is recorded in newspaper accounts as having given Annie a $5 piece that day.

What Does the Evidence Say?

Under ideal circumstances, I would load this chapter to the gills with illustrations so you could scrutinize each aspect and draw your own conclusions, but since that's not possible, I'll do my best to explain the analysis supplemented with a few key images. After more than another full year of research, here are the outcomes of the research strategies outlined above:

- If you take a close look at the photo, you'll notice that the other travelers in the background in the hall were dressed in long, heavy clothing—substantially different from the trio up front. An inspection of the passenger list for the *Nevada*, the small ship Annie and her brothers arrived on, showed that they were three of only eight Irish on board with the others being Russian and German. This would neatly explain the difference in attire.

- The girl in the photograph matches physical descriptions found in newspapers that covered the opening of Ellis Island. These included mentions that Annie was "bareheaded" (which would have stood out since the girl in the photo is the only one in the entire picture without a head covering of some sort), "buxom," and had a "woolly sack (jacket) buttoned closely about her." No conflicting descriptions were found.

- An *Irish World* article included a purported sketch of Annie that didn't look anything like the girl in the photo. However, the woman in the sketch also bears no resemblance to Annie in the pair of verified photos owned by family members. It shows a tall, slender, beak-nosed woman who appears considerably older than seventeen and is dressed in better clothing than most immigrants could afford. Nor does it match the descriptions of her in other articles since it depicts her with a head scarf tied under her chin, a long coat, and a purse and distinctive pouch that no one made any mention of.

- Maureen Taylor concluded that the three children are dressed in attire (e.g., "tight fitting cutaway jacket and cap with short pants," "knickered suit," etc.) that identifies them as being from the British Isles in the 1880s or early 1890s. She also underscored the fact that the children are separated from the rest with the others looking on, indicating that a special event is being captured. While she found the image quality too poor to conduct a facial analysis, she stated that there was "nothing in this image to prove a case against it being Annie and her brothers."

- The analysis conducted by forensic artist Stephen Mancusi also noted that the quality of the images was less than ideal, but that quite a few points of comparison were still available. In fact, his report delineated an impressive number of consistencies ranging from an "askew left iris" to a nose with a "slight snub quality." Though not requested to, he also felt compelled to comment on the "similar structure of all three subjects'

Excerpt from the forensic analysis conducted by Stephen Mancusi commissioned by the author.
(Image of possible Annie on left from Bob Hope Memorial Library at Ellis Island, of Annie in center from family of Anna [Moore] Shulman, and of Annie on right from Maureen Peterson)

hands." After taking proportions, individual features, and hands into account, he concluded that "this analysis points in one direction," and that "it is likely the female depicted in Image A is the same individual as the female depicted in B1 and B2, but at a younger age" (See the illustration).

- A close inspection of the photo with the three children showed pillars with a distinctive trio of braces (two solid

HARPER'S WEEKLY.   VOLUME XXXV., NO. 1818.

Harper's Weekly *included this image of the interior of the Barge Office in an 1891 issue. (Harper's Weekly)*

ones and one double one) at the top and walls with vertical panels stretching to the ceiling, so a logical question
was whether either the Barge Office or pre-fire Ellis Island
shared this unusual architecture. In today's world when
we're all awash in digital images, it's hard to imagine that
it would be challenging to find illustrations of the inside
of these two buildings, but it was surprisingly difficult.
With some effort, several of each were eventually tracked
down. The result? Three of the Barge Office (found in
1891 issues of *Harper's Weekly* and *Scribner's* magazines;
one from *Harper's* follows) looked completely different
from the room in which the children were standing.

• By contrast, those of the original Ellis Island facility consistently sported identical pillars and braces as those seen
in the photograph of the three children (see the following
illustration, which shows close-ups from an 1893 interior
sketch of Ellis Island [left] and from the photo being investigated [right]). Several 1897 pictures of Ellis Island
contributed by Marian Smith, senior historian of the U.S.

*The struts seen in the 1893 image of Ellis Island on the left
bear a striking similarity to those seen in the photo of the
youngsters.* (*Harper's Weekly* and Bob Hope Memorial
Library at Ellis Island)

Citizenship and Immigration Services, also featured the
same vertical wall panels. Similarly, the scale and architecture of the original Ellis Island (as found, for instance,
in an 1891 image of its construction) also mapped with
that of the large hall the young threesome was in. In
short, the visual evidence strongly indicates that the
photo in question was taken at Ellis Island and not, as
stated, at the Barge Office.

- I would be remiss if I did not point out one contradictory
  piece of information that cropped up during the course of
  this research. A new electronic file of the photo with the
  girl and two boys mysteriously materialized in early 2010.
  Though those who had seen it up until this point had all
  said that it had no caption, this version now included a
  label: "German-Russian woman Destination—Dakota
  Religion—Lutheran." What's odd about this is not only
  the singling out of the girl (why no mention of the boys?),
  but also that it, based on other resources, seems so con-
  spicuously wrong. For instance, Ellis Island librarian
  Barry Moreno's delightful, photo-laden book, *Images of*

America: Castle Garden and Battery Park, includes a pair of photographs of "English singing girls" and "Germans from Russia," both dated 1890, conveniently displayed across from each other on facing pages. Even with no prior knowledge of the topic, anyone viewing these two pictures could easily determine by looking at the clothing and hair styles which group the trio of children in the large hall belong to—and it's not the Germans. The English girls, for example, are all bare-headed with short jackets—just like the girl with the two boys—while the Germans from Russia look like those with the long, heavy clothing standing in the background of the photograph of the threesome. But the most telling moment was when I examined the pages of Weber's album. This label was indeed there, but attached to the same "Germans from Russia" image found in the book I just mentioned. Annie's great-nephew, Michael Shulman, had been right when he told me the photo of the three children had no label, so it was now clear that this recently appended caption was wrong. It pertained to an entirely different photo.

- Regrettably, none of the descendants of John B. Weber or Patrick McCool had additional pictures, but one of Weber's great-granddaughters remarked that he was a politician and would have been well aware of the importance of commemorating the opening of Ellis Island. Since that event is considered to be the highlight of Weber's tenure, it's clear why he would have wanted to include it in his collection.

- The notion of Weber's having reason to include this particular photo was reinforced when I inspected all the pages of his album. While most of them portrayed immigrants at the Barge Office, there was an evident logic to it, starting with the fact that Weber had placed himself

Superintendent Weber's before and after photos:
Barge Office on the left and Ellis Island on the right.
(Bob Hope Memorial Library at Ellis Island)

prominently at the beginning. Clearly, this was meant to
capture his time in charge. But what especially jumped
out was his before-and-after version of his service (see
the illustration). One page featured two photos—a top
one of an immigrant-laden steamer identified as "*Wm
Fletcher*" arriving at a dock with a second one under-
neath showing a mob of immigrants being processed in a
crowded registry hall. Handwritten labels specify that
both were taken at the Barge Office. This was the "before." Another page showed the same scenario, but this
time the passenger-heavy *Wm Fletcher* is seen arriving at
what is easily recognizable as Ellis Island. And the corresponding photo of immigrants in the registration hall?
It's the one this whole investigation had focused on. In
other words, these were the only two photos in the entire

album taken at Ellis Island, and as such, were meant to serve as the "after" shot demonstrating that Weber had successfully overseen the opening of Ellis Island.

Is It or Isn't It?

In all the research that was done, only three pieces of conflicting evidence emerged: 1) the sketch in the *Irish World*, 2) the assertion that the photo was taken at the Barge Office, and 3) a fresh caption. We can dismiss the first since we now know that Annie looked nothing like the Mary Poppins-esque woman in that sketch. To date, no substantiation has been offered for the Barge Office claim, which makes it highly suspect given that interior images found of the Barge Office look entirely different. What I believe happened is that someone jumped to this conclusion simply because the majority of the photos from Weber's album were of the Barge Office and failed to recognize the significance of the before-and-after pages. As to the peculiar caption, we realize now that it's an error.

On the other hand, there's a massive wall of evidence that supports the notion that this is the true Annie Moore. Provenance weighs in her favor, as does every other visual, descriptive, historical, forensic, and architectural analysis performed, starting with the fact that the threesome is the right combination of ages and genders to have been Annie and her brothers (and incidentally, all the research has failed to turn up any other such trios).

The simple fact that pictures of Annie in later years look so similar is important, as is the sequence of the discovery of the photographs. The odds were that these later photos should have been able to rule Annie out, but instead, they strengthened her case. Newspaper articles about that eventful day describe Annie dressed just as the girl in the photo. None of the painstakingly sought-out images of the Barge Office and the original Ellis Island dispute the possibility that the three youngsters were photographed at Ellis Island. In fact, they strongly support that locale over the Barge Office. Analyses by both a renowned historical photo expert and world-class forensic artist turned up nothing—whether hair, clothing, facial or hand details—that could eliminate Annie from consideration. Rather, the list of consistencies they detailed only served to bolster the growing pile of evidence.

I know what my conclusion is. What's yours?

Acknowledgments

If I were to thank everyone who has helped me with this book and the projects included in it, this portion would exceed the rest of the book, so I must regretfully single out just a few:

- If it weren't for both my editor, Michaela Hamilton, and literary agent, Linda Konner, you wouldn't be reading these words. Simply put, they both cared—far beyond what their responsibilities required—and that made all the difference in the world.

- While I have many friends in the genealogical world, Lou Szucs, Juliana Smith, Katherine Hope Borges, and Curt Witcher stand out as having been both champions of our beloved profession and beyond kind to me. Thank you for your friendship and for all you do for so many.

- Alyssa Gregory, Bev Miller, Sam Butterworth, and Sharon Elliott have supported me professionally and cheerfully put up with me for at least five years each. There should be some sort of endurance prize for that.

- Anna Harding has patiently coached me through more than a decade worth of highs and lows, starting with the then-scary transition from management consulting to genealogy.

- It amazes me that busy people like Henry Louis Gates, Jr., Ken Burns, and Stephen Colbert troubled to return my emails and I'm beyond grateful to each for his contribution, especially to Skip for his thoughtful foreword.

- Stacy Neuberger had no idea what was in store for her when fate assigned her the burden of being my sister, but all these years later, she still does it with a smile—even after painstakingly reviewing every single word of six books to date. It would take me more than another lifetime to balance out the sisterhood scales.

- I thank my lucky stars every day that I found and married Brian Smolenyak. He's one of those almost mythical "good guys" you hear about, and he's always got my back. Bri, you truly are one in seven billion and the only one for me.

Finally, I'd like to thank everyone who's ever let me peek into their ancestral past, read one of my articles or books, attended one of my talks, followed me on Twitter and Facebook, or virtually high-fived me in some way. You all make what I do even more fun than it already is!

Permissions

Grateful acknowledgment is made for the permission of Ancestry.com to reprint revised versions of previously published materials from *Ancestry Magazine*, specifically:

- "Serial Centenarians," July/August 2007.
- "The Man (or Woman) Who Would Be King," September/October 2008.

- "The Quest for Obama's Irish Roots," November/December 2008.
- "Philip Reed, The Slave Who Rescued Freedom," May/June 2009.
- "DNA Proves Scottish Roots of Haley Family," July/August 2009.

Index